Pelican Books
Encounter Groups

Carl Rogers is the Dean of the encounter-group movement. His life-long emphasis on client-centred therapy and on personal growth has been incorporated in the basic structure of *Encounter Groups*. He is the author of many articles and a number of books, which include *On Becoming a Person* (1961) and *Carl Rogers on Encounter Groups* (1970), and has received both of the major awards of the American Psychological Association. He is at present a Resident Fellow at the Center for Studies of the Person, La Jolla, California.

Carl R. Rogers

Encounter Groups

Penguin Books

Penguin Books Ltd, Harmondsworth,
Middlesex, England
Penguin Books Australia Ltd, Ringwood,
Victoria, Australia
Penguin Books (N.Z.) Ltd, 182–190
Wairau Road, Auckland 10, New Zealand

Carl Rogers on Encounter Groups
first published in the U.S.A. 1970

Published in Great Britain by Allen Lane
The Penguin Press 1969
Published in Pelican Books 1973
Reprinted 1974, 1975
Copyright © Carl R. Rogers, 1970

Made and printed in Great Britain by
Cox & Wyman Ltd, London, Reading and Fakenham
Set in Intertype Lectura

Contents

Foreword

For more than thirty-five years, individual counselling and psychotherapy were the main focus of my professional life. But nearly thirty-five years ago I also experienced the potency of the changes in attitudes and behaviour which could be achieved in a group. This has been an interest of mine ever since. However, only in the past seven or eight years has it become one of the two primary foci of my work – the other being the crucial need for greater freedom in our educational institutions.

During this latter time I have written papers and given talks on various facets of the burgeoning movement towards encounter groups. I am continually being asked questions about what happens in groups, about my way of working, about the implications of the whole movement.

So I decided to assemble for publication both the talks and papers I have given, together with new material written for this book, in the hope that they will stimulate a thoughtful analysis and a clarification of differences regarding this incredibly expanding trend.

As with all my more recent books, this is definitely a personal document. It does not pretend to be a scholarly survey of the field, nor a profound psychological or sociological analysis of encounter groups. It does not even indulge in much speculation as to the future of the encounter group, which I think is a sufficiently powerful force to carve its own ramifying future in its own way. This book is written out of living personal experience, and those whose lives are described and whose statements are quoted are living, struggling people. I hope it will convey *my* perception of one of the exciting developments of our time: the intensive group experience. And I hope it will help to familiarize you with what an encounter group *is*, and what it can *mean*.

I

The Origin and Scope of the Trend Towards 'Groups'

This title may seem odd. Clearly there always have been and always will be groups, as long as man survives on this planet. But I am using the word in a special sense, that of the planned, intensive group experience. This is, in my judgement, the most rapidly spreading *social* invention of the century, and probably the most potent – an invention that goes by many names. 'T-group', 'encounter groups', 'sensitivity training' are among the most common. Sometimes such groups are known as laboratories in human relationships, or workshops in leadership, education, or counselling. When it deals with drug addicts the group is often labelled a synanon, after the Synanon organization and its techniques.

One element which makes this phenomenon well worth psychological study is the fact that it has grown up entirely outside the 'establishment'. Most universities still look upon it with scorn. Until the last two or three years, foundations and government agencies have been unwilling to fund programmes of research in this area; the established professions of clinical psychology and psychiatry have stayed aloof, while the political right wing is certain that it represents a deep-seated Communist plot. I know of few other trends which have so clearly expressed the need and desire of *people* rather than institutions. In spite of such adverse pressures, the movement has blossomed and grown until it has permeated every part of the country and almost every kind of modern organization. It obviously has significant social implications. Part of the purpose of this chapter will be to look into some of the reasons for its surprisingly rapid and spontaneous growth.

These intensive groups have functioned in a variety of settings. They have operated in industries, in universities, in church settings; in government agencies, educational institutions, and penitentiaries. An astonishing range of individuals has been involved in this group experience. There have been groups for presidents of large corporations, and groups for delinquent and pre-delinquent adolescents. There have been groups composed of college students and faculty members, of counsellors and psychotherapists; of school drop-outs, of married couples, of families, including both parents and children; of confirmed drug addicts, of criminals serving sentences; of nurses, educators, teachers, school administrators, industrial managers, State Department ambassadors – even members of the Internal Revenue Service!

The geographical spread attained by this rapidly expanding movement has reached from Bethel, Maine, to San Diego, California, and from Seattle to Palm Beach. Intensive groups have also been conducted in a number of other countries, including England, France, Holland, Australia, and Japan.

Origin

Some time prior to 1947 Kurt Lewin, a famous psychologist working at the Massachusetts Institute of Technology with his staff and students, developed the idea that training in human relations skills was an important but overlooked type of education in modern society. The first so-called T-group (T standing for training) was held in Bethel, Maine in 1947, shortly after Lewin's death. Those who had worked with him continued to develop these training groups, both while they were at MIT and later at the University of Michigan. The summer groups at Bethel came to be well known. An organization, the National Training Laboratories, was formed, with offices in Washington, D.C., which has steadily grown throughout more than two decades since that time. The primary thrust of the NTL groups has been in the industrial field, reaching managers and executives. This direction developed primarily because industry could afford the expense of such group experience for its top personnel.

The groups initially fitted the T-group description of their name. They were training groups in human relations skills in which individuals were taught to observe the nature of their interactions with others and of the group process. From this, it was felt, they would be better able to understand their own way of functioning in a group and on the job, and the impact they had on others, and would become more competent in dealing with difficult interpersonal situations.

In the T-groups organized by NTL for industry, and gradually in many areas outside of industry, it was found that individuals often had very deep personal experiences of change in the trusting, caring relationship that grew up among the participants.

Another phase of the movement towards intensive group experience was developing at about the same time at the University of Chicago. In 1946 and 1947, immediately after World War II, my associates and I at the Counseling Center of the University of Chicago were involved in training personal counsellors for the Veterans Administration. We were asked to create a brief but intensive course of training which would prepare these men – all of whom had at least a master's degree – to become effective personal counsellors in dealing with the problems of returning GIs. Our staff felt that no amount of cognitive training would prepare them, so we experimented with an intensive group experience in which the trainees met for several hours each day in order better to understand themselves, to become aware of attitudes which might be self-defeating in the counselling relationship, and to relate to each other in ways that would be helpful and could carry over into their counselling work. This was an attempt to tie together experiential and cognitive learning in a process which had therapeutic value for the individual. It provided many deep and meaningful experiences for the trainees, and was so successful in a sequence of groups of personal counsellors that our staff continued to use the procedure in summer workshops thereafter.

There was no attempt by our Chicago group to expand this approach, and it is worth mentioning only because the somewhat different emphasis represented in the Chicago experience has gradually become embedded in the whole movement involving intensive group experience. The Chicago groups were oriented primarily towards personal growth and the development and improvement of interpersonal communication and relationships, rather than having these as secondary aims. They also had more of an experiential and therapeutic orientation than the groups originating in Bethel. Over the years this orientation towards personal and therapeutic growth has become merged with the focus of training in human relations skills, and the two combined form the core of the trend which is spreading so rapidly throughout the country today.

Thus the conceptual underpinnings of this whole movement were initially Lewinian thinking and Gestalt psychology on the one hand, and client-centred therapy on the other. In recent years many other theories and influences have played a part.

Differing Emphases and Forms

As interest in the intensive group experience, and use of it, has grown, spread, and multiplied, there has developed a wide diversity of emphases. The following list with its brief descriptive phrases certainly oversimplifies the situation, but may give some idea of the broad spectrum involved.

T-group. As indicated above, this originally tended to emphasize human relations *skills* but has become much broader in its approach.

Encounter group (or basic encounter group). This tends to emphasize personal growth and the development and improvement of interpersonal communication and relationships through an experiential process.

Sensitivity training group. May resemble either of the above.

Task-oriented group. Widely used in industry. Focuses on the task of the group in its interpersonal context.

Sensory awareness groups, body awareness groups, body movement groups. As the labels indicate, these tend to emphasize physical awareness and expression through movement, spontaneous dance, and the like.

Creativity workshops. Here creative expression through various art media often forms the focus, with individual spontaneity and freedom of expression the aim.

Organizational development group. The primary aim is growth in skill as a leader of persons.

Team building group. Used in industry to develop more closely knit and effective working teams.

Gestalt group. Emphasis on a Gestalt therapeutic approach where an expert therapist focuses on one individual at a time, but from a diagnostic and therapeutic point of view.

Synanon group or 'game'. Developed in the treatment of drug addicts by the Synanon organization. Tends to emphasize almost violent attack on the defences of the participants.

In addition to this partial list one might mention some of the different *forms* that may be found. There are 'stranger groups' composed of individuals unacquainted with each other. There are staff groups from one organization, people associated in their everyday life in industry, education, or whatever their occupational setting may be. There are large workshops or 'labs' in which a number of small groups may be conducted simultaneously, each maintaining its own continuity, while the whole workshop often gets together for some common experience such as a talk or other cognitive session. One may find couples' groups, in which married couples meet with the hope of helping each other improve their marital relationships. A recent development is the family group, where several families join in one group, with parents learning from their own and others' children and vice versa.

Then there are differences in the time element. Most groups meet intensively during a week-end, a week, or several weeks. In some instances group sessions are held once or twice a week. There are also marathon groups which meet continuously for twenty-four hours or more.[1]

Threads in Common

Simply to describe the diversity in this field raises very properly the question of why these various developments should be con-

1. It might be mentioned in passing that 'nude marathons' in which people may divest themselves of their clothes have received an enormous amount of publicity, although they certainly constitute less than one-tenth of one per cent of intensive group experiences.

sidered as belonging together at all. Are there any common threads running through all these widely divergent activities and emphases? To me it seems that they do belong together and may all be classed as focusing on the intensive group experience. They all tend to have certain similar external characteristics. The group in almost every case is small (from eight to eighteen members), relatively unstructured, choosing its own goals and personal directions. The experience often, though not always, includes some cognitive input – some content material which is presented to the group. In almost all instances the leader's responsibility is primarily the facilitation of the expression of both feelings and thoughts on the part of group members. Both in the leader and in the members there is a focus on the process and dynamics of immediate personal interactions. These are, I believe, some of the identifying characteristics which are rather easily recognized.

There are also certain practical hypotheses which tend to be held in common by all these groups, which might be formulated in quite different ways. Here is one such formulation.

A facilitator can develop, in a group which meets intensively, a psychological climate of safety in which freedom of expression and reduction of defensiveness gradually occur.

In such a psychological climate many of the immediate feeling reactions of each member towards others, and of each member towards himself, tend to be expressed.

A climate of mutual trust develops out of this mutual freedom to express real feelings, positive and negative. Each member moves towards greater acceptance of his total being – emotional, intellectual, and physical – as it *is*, including its potential.

With individuals less inhibited by defensive rigidity, the possibility of change in personal attitudes and behaviour, in professional methods, in administrative procedures and relationships, becomes less threatening.

With the reduction of defensive rigidity, individuals can hear each other, can learn from each other, to a greater extent.

There is a development of feedback from one person to

another, such that each individual learns how he appears to others and what impact he has in interpersonal relationships.

With this greater freedom and improved communication, new ideas, new concepts, new directions emerge. Innovation can become a desirable rather than a threatening possibility.

These learnings in the group experience tend to carry over, temporarily or more permanently, into the relationships with spouse, children, students, subordinates, peers, and even superiors following the group experience.

While this description of basic aspects of the experience would probably fit a majority of groups, it would be less applicable in such situations as Gestalt therapy and other groups where the leader is much more in charge and much more manipulative.

It might be mentioned that the style of the leader and his own concepts of the group process make a great deal of difference in the conduct and experience of the group. It has been found however that in leaderless groups, where individuals simply meet intensively without any one person named as facilitator or leader, the process that occurs is similar to the description given. Hence, it might be said that variations from it often depend on the style or point of view of the leader or facilitator.

The Group Process

In the following chapter I shall try to give a somewhat detailed picture of the group process, but a very brief and general overview will be appropriate here.

Because of the unstructured nature of the group, the major problem faced by the participants is how they are going to use their time together – whether it be eighteen hours of a weekend or forty or more hours in a one-week group. Often there is consternation, anxiety, and irritation at first – particularly because of the lack of structure. Only gradually does it become evident that the major aim of nearly every member is to find ways of relating to other members of the group and to himself.

Then as they gradually, tentatively, and fearfully explore their feelings and attitudes towards one another and towards themselves, it becomes increasingly evident that what they have first presented are façades, masks. Only cautiously do the real feelings and real persons emerge. The contrast between the outer shell and the inner person becomes more and more apparent as the hours go by. Little by little, a sense of genuine communication builds up, and the person who has been thoroughly walled off from others comes out with some small segment of his actual feelings. Usually his attitude has been that his real feelings will be quite unacceptable to other members of the group. To his astonishment, he finds that he is more accepted the more real that he becomes. Negative feelings are often especially feared, since it seems certain to each individual that his angry or jealous feelings cannot possibly be accepted by another. Thus one of the most common developments is that a sense of trust slowly begins to build, and also a sense of warmth and liking for other members of the group. A woman says on Sunday afternoon, 'If anybody had told me Friday evening that by today I would be loving every member of this group I would have told him that he belonged in the nut house.' Participants feel a closeness and intimacy which they have not felt even with their spouses or members of their own family, because they have revealed themselves here more deeply and more fully than to those in their own family circle.

Thus, in such a group the individual comes to know himself and each of the others more completely than is possible in the usual social or working relationships. He becomes deeply acquainted with the other members and with his own inner self, the self that otherwise tends to be hidden behind his façade. Hence he relates better to others, both in the group and later in the everyday life situation.

Why the Rapid Spread?

It would be difficult to find a medium- to large-sized city in our country today in which some sort of intensive group experience is not available. The rapidity of the spread of interest has been incredible. A year or so ago, when I was about to speak to a large general audience in a western city, I asked the man responsible for organizing the meeting what proportion of the audience would have had some experience in an encounter group or something similar. He gave as his answer, 'Less than a third.' After giving a brief description of such a group and the various labels attached to it, I asked for a show of hands of those who had experienced such a group. About three-fourths of the audience of twelve hundred raised their hands. I am sure that ten years ago hardly fifty people could have so responded.

One factor which makes the rapidity of the spread even more remarkable is its complete and unorganized spontaneity. Contrary to the shrill voices of the right wing (whom I will mention below), this has not been a 'conspiracy'. Quite the contrary. No group or organization has been pushing the development of encounter groups. There has been no financing of such a spread, either from foundations or governments. Many orthodox psychologists and psychiatrists have frowned upon the development. Yet in spite of this, in churches, colleges, 'growth centres', and industry the number of groups has burgeoned. It has been a spontaneous demand, by people clearly seeking something. As an example, some of the staff members of our Center for Studies of the Person conduct a summer programme for the training of group facilitators or leaders. As a part of the programme they provide the opportunity for pairs of trainees to co-lead two groups on successive week-ends. To procure participants for these groups they have sent out announcements to a modest mailing-list, almost entirely in the San Diego area. There has been no paid publicity or even newspaper items about the opportunity. The only unusual inducement was that participants had to pay only for their registration and board and room. There was no 'tuition' charge, since it was openly stated that the facilitators were persons in training. Initially I predicted that with so little publicity they would fail to enroll an adequate number. To my amazement, six hundred people signed up for the first weekend, and eight hundred for the second. This indicates a spontaneous grass-roots demand of unbelievable strength and size.

What accounts for the quick spread of groups? For the enormous demand? I believe the soil out of which this demand grows has two elements. The first is the increasing dehumanization of our culture, where the person does not count – only his IBM card or Social Security number. This impersonal quality runs through all the institutions in our land. The second element is that we are sufficiently affluent to pay attention to our psychological wants. As long as I am concerned over next month's rent, I am not very sharply aware of my loneliness. This is borne out, in my experience, by the fact that interest in encounter groups and the like is not nearly so keen in ghetto areas as in sections of the population which are no longer so concerned about the physical necessities of life.

But what is the psychological need that draws people into encounter groups? I believe it is a hunger for something the person does not find in his work environment, in his church, certainly not in his school or college, and, sadly enough, not even in modern family life. It is a hunger for relationships which are close and real; in which feelings and emotions can be spontaneously expressed without first being carefully censored or bottled up; where deep experiences – disappointments and joys – can be shared; where new ways of behaving can be risked and tried out; where, in a word, he approaches the state where all is known and all accepted, and thus further growth becomes possible. This seems to be the overpowering hunger which he hopes to satisfy through his experiences in an encounter group.

Fear Created by the Trend

All types of intensive group experience have come under the most virulent attack from right-wing and reactionary groups. It is, to them, a form of 'brainwashing' and 'thought control'. It is both a Communist conspiracy and a Nazi plot. The statements made are ludicrously extreme and often contradictory. It is fair to say that it is often pictured as being one of the greatest dangers threatening our country.

As usual in such attacks, a small amount of truthful reporting is mingled with frightening conclusions and innuendo.

Thus Congressman Rarick read into the Congressional Record of 19 January 1970 a diatribe by Ed Dieckmann, Jr entitled 'Sensitivity International – Network for World Control'. One of the milder sections, illustrative of the technique, is as follows:

On September 23 1968 the then President of the NEA, Elizabeth D. Koontz . . . said . . .

'The NEA has a multi-faceted program already directed toward the urban school problem embracing every phase, from the Headstart Program to sensitivity training for adults – both teachers and parents.'

Thus she revealed the real goal: involvement of the entire community in one gigantic laboratory of groups exactly as in North Vietnam, Russia and Red China.

It is enlightening to know that this same Elizabeth Koontz the first Negro president of the NEA and a known member of the board of SIECUS the infamous 'Sex Information & Education Council for the U.S.,' was appointed by President Nixon earlier this year Director of the Women's Bureau of the Department of Labor!

Synchronized with the attack by what we must remember is 'coercive persuasion or brainwashing', was the announcement last February by New York University that it now offers a master's degree in sensitivity training; followed by Redlands University in California with its trumpet blast in May that it, too, starts ST this summer – and that it will be mandatory!

Here a bona fide quotation – quite sensible – is made to serve as a base for utterly unfounded assertions and a vaguely horrendous innuendo.

Another right-wing writer, Alan Stang, in *The Review of the News* for 9 April 1969 (p. 16) inquires of his readers, 'Aren't our teachers being subjected to "sensitivity training" to prepare them for the dictatorial control which is the essence of Nazism and all Socialism?' Another article by Gary Allen in *American Opinion*, official organ of the John Birch Society (January 1968, p. 73) carries its message in its title: 'Hate Therapy: Sensitivity Training for Planned Change.' He asserts that sensitivity training is '. . . now being promoted throughout the country by the usual forces of the conspiratorial Left.'

One could go on and on, citing much more extreme statements which issue in a flood from the far right. It is very clear that sensitivity groups, encounter groups, and any other form of the intensive group experience, are for them the bête noire of American society.

James Harmon, in a carefully documented study, concludes that there is ample evidence that the right wing has a large proportion of authoritarian personalities.[2] They tend to believe that man is, by nature, basically evil. Surrounded as all of us are by the bigness of impersonal forces which seem beyond our power to control, they look for 'the enemy', so that they can hate him. At different times in history 'the enemy' has been the witch, the demon, the Communist (remember Joe McCarthy?), and now sex education, sensitivity training, 'nonreligious humanism', and other current demons.

My own explanation is more in line with Harmon's second conclusion. Putting it in my own words: encounter groups lead to more personal independence, fewer hidden feelings, more willingness to innovate, more opposition to institutional rigidities. Hence, if a person is fearful of change in any form, he is rightly fearful of encounter groups. They breed constructive change, as will be evident in the chapters that follow. Hence, all those who are opposed to change will be stoutly or even violently opposed to the intensive group experience.

CONCLUSION

I have endeavoured to place in historical perspective the surging development and use of the intensive group experience, sketching briefly some of the forms and emphases which are currently observable. I have tried to indicate the humanizing elements that tend to characterize such groups, and have suggested a possible explanation for the rapid growth of this trend and why it is so feared by those who oppose change. Perhaps we are now ready to examine at closer range the events that tend to occur in such a group.

2. James E. Harmon, 'Ideological Aspects of Right-Wing Criticism of the Intensive Group Experience'. Unpublished paper written for a seminar in human behaviour, May 1969.

2

The Process of the Encounter Group[1]

What really goes on in an encounter group? This is a question often asked by persons who are contemplating joining one, or who are puzzled by the statements of people who have had the experience. The question has been of great interest to me also, as I have tried to understand what appear to be common elements in the group experience. I have come to sense, at least dimly, some of the patterns or stages a group seems to go through and will describe them as best I can.

My formulation is simple and naturalistic. I am not attempting to build a high-level abstract theory,[2] nor to make profound interpretations of unconscious motives or of some developing group psyche. You will not find me speaking of group myths, or even of dependence and counter-dependence. I am not comfortable with such inferences, correct though they may be. At this stage of our knowledge I wish merely to describe the observable events and the way in which, to me, these

---

1. Much of the material in this chapter was published in abbreviated form in a chapter of *Challenges of Humanistic Psychology*, ed. J. F. T. Bugental (London and New York: McGraw Hill Book Company, 1967), and also in *Psychology Today*, Vol. 3, No. 7 (December 1969).

2. Jack and Lorraine Gibb have long been working on an analysis of trust development as the essential theory of group process. Others who have contributed significantly to the theory of group process are Chris Argyris, Kenneth Benne, Warren Bennis, Robert Blake, Dorwin Cartwright, Matthew Miles. Samples of the thinking of all these and others may be found in the following books: *T-Group Theory and Laboratory Method*, ed. Bradford, Gibb, and Benne (New York: John Wiley and Sons, 1964); *The Planning of Change*, ed. Bennis, Benne, and Chin (London and New York: Holt, Rinehart, and Winston, 1961); and *Interpersonal Dynamics*, ed. Bennis, Schein, Berlew, and Steele (London: The Dorsey Press, 1968). Thus there are many promising leads for theory construction involving a considerable degree of abstraction. This chapter has a more elementary aim: a naturalistic descriptive account of the process.

events seem to cluster. In doing so I am drawing on my own experience and that of others with whom I have worked, upon written material in this field, upon the written reactions of many individuals who have participated in such groups, and to some extent upon recordings of such group sessions, which we are only beginning to tap and analyse.

As I consider the terribly complex interactions that arise in twenty, forty, or sixty or more hours of intensive sessions, I believe I see certain threads which weave in and out of the pattern. Some of these trends or tendencies are likely to appear early, some later in the group sessions, but there is no clear-cut sequence in which one ends and another begins. The interaction is best thought of, I believe, as a rich and varied tapestry, differing from group to group, yet with certain kinds of trends evident in most of these intensive encounters and with certain patterns tending to precede and others to follow. Here are some of the process patterns I see developing, briefly described in simple terms, illustrated from tape recordings and personal reports and presented in roughly sequential order.

1. *Milling around*. As the leader or facilitator makes clear at the outset that this is a group with unusual freedom and not one for which he will take directional responsibility, there tends to develop a period of initial confusion, awkward silence, polite surface interaction, 'cocktail-party talk', frustration, and great lack of continuity. The individuals come face to face with the fact that 'there is no structure here except what we provide. We do not know our purposes, we do not even know each other, and we are committed to remain together over a considerable period of time.' In this situation, confusion and frustration are natural. Particularly striking to the observer is the lack of continuity between personal expressions. Individual A will present some proposal or concern, clearly looking for a response from the group. Individual B has obviously been waiting for his turn and starts off on some completely different tangent as though he had never heard A. One member makes a simple suggestion such as, 'I think we should introduce ourselves,' and this may lead to several hours of highly involved discussion in which the underlying issues appear to be: Who

will tell us what to do? Who is responsible for us? What is the purpose of the group?

2. *Resistance to personal expression or exploration.* During the milling-around period some individuals are likely to reveal rather personal attitudes. This tends to provoke a very ambivalent reaction among other members of the group. One member, writing of his experience afterwards, says, 'There is a self which I present to the world and another one which I know more intimately. With others I try to appear able, knowing, unruffled, problem-free. To substantiate this image I will act in a way which at the time or later seems false or artificial or "not the real me". Or I will keep to myself thoughts which if expressed would reveal an imperfect me.

'My inner self, by contrast with the image I present to the world, is characterized by many doubts. The worth I attach to this inner self is subject to much fluctuation and is very dependent on how others are reacting to me. At times this private self can feel worthless.'

It is the public self that members tend to show each other, and only gradually, fearfully, and ambivalently do they take steps to reveal something of the private self.

Early in one intensive workshop, the members were asked to write anonymously a statement of some feeling or feelings they had which they were not willing to tell in the group. One man wrote, 'I don't relate easily to people. I have an almost impenetrable façade. Nothing gets in to hurt me but nothing gets out. I have repressed so many emotions that I am close to emotional sterility. This situation doesn't make me happy but I don't know what to do about it.' This individual is clearly living in a private dungeon, but except in this disguised fashion he does not even dare to send out a call for help.

In a recent workshop, when one man started to express the concern he felt about an impasse he was experiencing with his wife, another member stopped him, saying essentially, 'Are you sure you want to go on with this, or are you being seduced by the group into going further than you want to go? How do you know the group can be trusted? How will you feel about it when you go home and tell your wife what you have revealed, or when you decide to keep it from her? It just isn't safe to go further.' It seemed quite clear that in his warning this second member was also expressing his own fear of revealing *himself*, and *his* lack of trust in the group.

3. *Description of past feelings*. In spite of ambivalence about the trustworthiness of the group, and the risk of exposing oneself, expression of feelings does begin to assume a larger proportion of the discussion. The executive tells how frustrated he feels by certain situations in his industry; the housewife relates problems she has with her children. A tape-recorded exchange involving a Roman Catholic nun occurs early in a one-week workshop, when talk has turned to a rather intellectualized discussion of anger:

Bill: What happens when you get mad, Sister, or don't you?
Sister: Yes, I do – yes I do. And I find when I get mad, I, I almost get, well, the kind of person that antagonizes me is the person who seems so unfeeling toward people – now I take our dean as a person in point because she is a very aggressive woman and has certain ideas about what the various rules in a college should be; and this woman can just send me into high 'G'; in an angry mood. *I mean this*. But then I find, I . . .
Facilitator[3]: But what, what do you do?
Sister: I find that when I'm in a situation like this, I strike out in a very sharp *tone* or else I refuse to respond – 'all right, this happens to be her way' – I don't think I've ever gone into a tantrum.
Joe: You just withdraw – no use to fight it.
Facilitator: You say you use a sharp tone. To *her*, or to other people you're dealing with?
Sister: Oh no! To *her*.

This is a typical example of a *description* of feelings which in a sense are obviously current in her but which she is placing in the past and describes as being outside the group in time and place. It is an example of feelings existing 'there and then'.

4. *Expression of negative feelings*. Curiously enough, the

3. Sometimes referred to as a leader or trainer, for this person the term facilitator is most used in this book.

first expression of genuinely significant 'here and now' feeling is apt to come out in negative attitudes towards other group members or the group leader. In one group in which members introduced themselves at some length, one woman refused, saying that she preferred to be known for what she was in the group and not in terms of her status outside. Very shortly after this, a man in the group attacked her vigorously and angrily for this stand, accusing her of failing to cooperate, of keeping herself aloof from the group, of being unreasonable. It was the first *current personal feeling* brought into the open in that group.

Frequently the leader is attacked for his failure to give proper guidance. One vivid example of this comes from a recorded account of an early session with a group of delinquents, where one member shouts at the leader, 'You'll be licked if you don't control us right at the start. You have to keep order here because you are older than us. That's what a teacher is supposed to do. If he doesn't do it we'll make a lot of trouble and won't get anything done.' Then, referring to two boys in the group who were scuffling, he continues: 'Throw 'em out, throw 'em out! You've just *got* to make us behave!'[4]

An adult expresses his disgust at people who talk too much, but points his irritation at the leader. 'It's just that I don't understand why someone doesn't shut them up. I would have taken Gerald and shoved him out the window. I'm an authoritarian. I would have told him he was talking too much and he had to leave the room. I think the group discussion ought to be led by a person who simply will not recognize these people after they've interrupted about eight times.'[5]

Why are negatively toned expressions the first current feelings to be expressed? Some speculative answers might be the following. This is one of the best ways to test the freedom and trustworthiness of the group. Is it *really* a place where I can be and express myself, positively and negatively? Is this *really* a safe place, or will I be punished? Another quite different reason is that deeply positive feelings are much more difficult and dangerous to express than negative ones. If I say I love you, I am

4. T. Gordon, *Group-Centered Leadership* (Boston: Houghton Mifflin & Co., 1955), p. 214.
5. ibid., p. 210.

vulnerable and open to the most awful rejection. If I say I hate you, I am at best liable to attack, against which I can defend. Whatever the reasons, such negatively toned feelings tend to be the first 'here and now' material to appear.

5. *Expression and exploration of personally meaningful material*. It may seem puzzling that, following such negative experiences as the initial confusion, the resistance to personal expression, the focus on outside events, and the voicing of critical or angry feelings, the event most likely to occur next is for some individual to reveal himself to the group in a significant way. The reason for this no doubt is that the individual member has come to realize that this is in part *his group*. He can help to make of it what he wishes. He has also experienced the fact that negative feelings have been expressed and accepted or assimilated without catastrophic results. He realizes there is a freedom here, albeit a risky freedom. A climate of trust is beginning to develop. So he begins to take the chance and the gamble of letting the group know some deeper facet of himself. One man tells of the trap in which he finds himself, feeling that communication between himself and his wife is hopeless. A priest tells of the anger he has bottled up because of unreasonable treatment by one of his superiors. What should he have done? What might he do now? A scientist at the head of a large research department finds the courage to speak of his painful isolation, to tell the group that he has never had a single *friend* in his life. By the time he finishes, he is letting loose some of the tears of sorrow for himself which I am sure he has held in for many years. A psychiatrist tells of the guilt he feels because of the suicide of one of his patients. A man of forty tells of his absolute inability to free himself from the grip of his controlling mother. A process which one workshop member has called 'a journey to the centre of self', often a very painful process, has begun. A recorded example of such exploration is found in a statement by Sam, member of a one-week workshop. Someone had spoken of his strength.

Sam: Perhaps I am not aware of or experiencing it that way, as strength. (Pause) I think, when I was talking with, I think it was the first day, I was talking to you, Tom, when in the course of that, I expressed the *genuine surprise* I had, the first time I realized that I could *frighten* someone – It really, it was a discovery that I had to just kind of look at and feel and get to know, you know, it was such a *new* experience for me. I was so used to the feeling of being frightened by *others* that it had never occurred to me that anyone could be – I guess it *never had* – that anyone could be frightened of *me*. And I guess maybe it has something to do with how I feel about myself.

Such exploration is not always an easy process, nor is the whole group receptive to such self-revelation. In a group of institutionalized adolescents, all of whom have been in difficulty of one sort or another, one boy reveals an important aspect of himself and is immediately met by both acceptance and sharp non-acceptance from other members.

George: This is the thing. I've got too many problems at home – um, I think some of you know why I'm here, what I was charged with.

Mary: I don't.

Facilitator: Do you want to tell us?

George: Well – uh – it's sort of embarrassing.

Carol: Come on, it won't be so bad.

George: Well, I raped my sister. That's the only problem I have at home and I've overcome that, I think. (Rather long pause.)

Freda: Oooh, that's weird!

Mary: People have problems, Freda, I mean ya know . . .

Freda: Yeah, I know, but *yeOUW!!!*

Facilitator: (To Freda) You know about these problems, but they still are weird to you.

George: You see what I mean; it's embarrassing to talk about it.

Mary: Yeah, but it's OK.

George: It *hurts* to talk about it, but I know I've got to so I won't be guilt-ridden for the rest of my life.

Clearly Freda is completely shutting him out psychologically, while Mary in particular is showing a deep acceptance. George is definitely willing to take the risk.

6. *The expression of immediate interpersonal feelings in the group*. Entering into the process, sometimes earlier, sometimes later, is the explicit bringing into the open of feelings experienced in the immediate moments by one member towards another. These are sometimes positive, sometimes negative. Examples would be: 'I feel threatened by your silence.' 'You remind me of my mother, with whom I had a tough time.' 'I took an instant dislike to you the first moment I saw you.' 'To me you're like a breath of fresh air in the group.' 'I like your warmth and your smile.' 'I dislike you more every time you speak up.' Each of these attitudes can be, and usually is, explored in the increasing climate of trust.

7. *The development of a healing capacity in the group*. One of the most fascinating aspects of any intensive group experience is to observe the manner in which a number of the group members show a natural and spontaneous capacity for dealing in a helpful, facilitating, and therapeutic fashion with the pain and suffering of others. As one rather extreme example of this I think of a man in charge of maintenance in a large plant who was one of the low-status members of an industrial executive group. As he informed us, he had 'not been contaminated by education'. In the initial phases the group tended to look down on him. As members delved more deeply into themselves and began to express their own attitudes more fully, this man came forth as without doubt the most sensitive member of the group. He knew intuitively how to be understanding and accepting. He was alert to things which had not yet been expressed but were just below the surface. While the rest of us were paying attention to a member who was speaking, he would frequently spot another individual who was suffering silently and in need of help. He had a deeply perceptive and facilitating attitude. This kind of ability shows up so commonly in groups that it has led me to feel that the ability to be healing or therapeutic is far more common in human life than we suppose. Often it needs only the permission granted – or freedom made possible – by the climate of a free-flowing group experience to become evident.

Here is a characteristic instance of the leader and several group members trying to help Joe, who has been telling of the almost complete lack of communication between himself and his wife. A lengthy excerpt from the recorded session seems justified, since it shows in what varied ways members endeavour to give help. John keeps putting before him the feelings his wife is almost certainly experiencing. The facilitator keeps challenging his façade of carefulness. Marie tries to help him discover what he is feeling at the moment. Fred shows him the choice he has of alternative behaviours. All this is clearly done in a spirit of caring, as is even more evident in the recording itself. No miracles are achieved, but towards the end Joe does come to realize that the only thing that might help would be to *express* his *real feelings* to his wife.

Joe: I've got to be real careful when I go somewhere if I know a lot of people and do things, so that my wife just doesn't feel that she's left out; and of course, I – things have changed so in the last year that I have hope, but for a while I *didn't*. I don't know whether we can break through it or not. (Pause.)

John: It comes to me over and over again that she wants very much to get inside – inside you.

Joe: She does.

John: I, I didn't mean in a hurting way, I mean . . .

Joe: No. (Pause.) But it's how to do it. And gosh, I've gotta let her in; but gosh, I've also gotta be so *careful* and the chances don't come very often . . .

Facilitator: Do you feel you got somewhere in this group by being careful? (Pause.)

Joe: Well, I've been pretty hard the other way here. In other words I think we haven't been careful here at all.

Facilitator: I don't either. I think you've taken a lot of risks.

Joe: What I meant by being careful is, I've gotta be careful about how I say anything or it's twisted on me.

Facilitator: If – well, I guess I'll be more blunt. If you think she can't tell when you're being very careful, you're *nuts*.

Joe: Yeah, I agree.

Facilitator: And if somebody approaches me – and I feel they're moving very gingerly and carefully, then I wonder, what's he trying to put over on me?

Joe: Well, I've tried it the other way – the worst thing is – maybe, to begin with I was too blunt. That's when we got into our arguments.

Facilitator: Yeah, but it sounds – I really appreciate the risk you're taking, or the trust you're putting in us to tell us about this kind of situation. Yet you start talking about the elements *outside* of yourself.

John: I keep wanting to ask if you can *feel* her feelings?

Joe: Well, uh, now – feelings, I, yes I'm getting so I can feel her feelings much more and – uh I – uh – the thing that bothered me was I remembered some feelings that she wanted to come in, and at that time I turned her down. Now that's where I got turned off. And – but I can feel right away when she's upset and so then I – well I don't know – you see then I . . .

Facilitator: What does that do to your feelings? Suppose you come home and you find that she's quiet, because you've been away and she's wondering about what has been going on and she's quite upset. What's that going to make *you* feel?

Joe: Uh – a tendency to withdraw.

Marie: What would you be feeling – withdrawal? Or would you be feeling upset, or maybe even anger?

Joe: I did before – not now so much – I can get that pretty much. I've watched that pretty carefully.

Marie: Yes, but that isn't my question, Joe.

Joe: All right.

Marie: I'm not asking if you can control it or push it away. What will the *feeling* be there?

Joe: Uh – I'm pretty much at the place now where it's just sort of withdrawal and wait; and I know if I can get by that evening, it'll be different tomorrow morning.

Fred: Do you feel it might be defensive, and do you express this defence in withdrawing because . . .

Joe: Well, she doesn't like it.

Fred: But you like it *less* this way than getting involved in an argument or disagreement?

Joe: Yeah – because the only thing that might work is – is if I *just expressed the feeling*. And I hope that'll make a difference – that 'I resented what you just said' or something like that, because before I would *answer* her, and boy, it was off! *That just didn't work*, and then she would always say I started it – but *with my being so conscious* now of when she's upset – I mean – I've got that real clear, and I just haven't known how to handle it.

Clearly each of these several individuals is trying in his own way to help, to heal, to form a helping relationship with Joe so as to enable him to deal with his wife in a more constructive, more real way.

8. *Self-acceptance and the beginning of change.* Many people feel that self-acceptance must stand in the way of change. Actually, in these group experiences as in psychotherapy, it is the *beginning* of change.

Some examples of the kinds of attitude expressed would be these: 'I *am* a dominating person who likes to control others. I do want to mould these individuals into the proper shape.' 'I really have a hurt and overburdened little boy inside of me who feels very sorry for himself. I *am* that little boy, in addition to being a competent and responsible manager.'

I think of one government executive, a man with high responsibility and excellent technical training as an engineer. At the first meeting of the group he impressed me, and I think others, as being cold, aloof, somewhat bitter, resentful, cynical. When he spoke of how he ran his office he appeared to administer it 'by the book' without warmth or human feeling entering in. In one of the early sessions, when he spoke of his wife a group member asked him, 'Do you love your wife?' He paused for a long time, and the questioner said, 'OK, that's answer enough.' The executive said, 'No, wait a minute! The reason I didn't respond was that I was wondering if I ever loved anyone. I don't think I have *ever* really *loved* anyone.' It seemed quite dramatically clear to those of us in the group that he had come to accept himself as an unloving person.

A few days later he listened with great intensity as one member of the group expressed profound personal feelings of isolation, loneliness, pain, and the extent to which he had been living behind a mask, a façade. The next morning the engineer said, 'Last night I thought and thought about what Bill told us. I even wept quite a bit by myself. I can't remember how long it has been since I've cried and I really *felt* something. I think perhaps what I felt was love.'

It is not surprising that before the week was over he had thought through new ways of handling his growing son, on whom he had been placing extremely rigorous demands. He had also begun genuinely to appreciate his wife's love for him, which he now felt he could in some measure reciprocate.

Another recorded excerpt, from an adolescent group, shows a combination of self-acceptance and self-exploration. Art has been talking about his 'shell', and here he is beginning to work with the problems of accepting himself and also the façade he ordinarily exhibits.

Art: When that shell's on it's, uh . . .

Lois: It's on!

Art: Yeah, it's on tight.

Susan: Are you always so closed in when you're in your shell?

Art: No, I'm so darn used to living with the shell, it doesn't even bother me. I don't even know the real me. I think I've, well, I've pushed the shell away more here. When I'm out of my shell — only twice — once just a few minutes ago — I'm really me, I guess. But then I just sort of pull in a cord after me when I'm in my shell, and that's almost all the time. And I leave the front standing outside when I'm back in the shell.

Facilitator: And nobody's back in there with you?

Art: (Crying) Nobody else is in there with me, just me. I just pull everything into the shell and roll the shell up and shove it in my pocket. I take the shell, and the real me, and put it in my pocket where it's safe. I guess that's really the way I do it — I go into my shell and turn off the real world. And here — that's what I want to do here in this group, y' know — come out of my shell and actually throw it away.

Lois: You're making progress already. At least you can talk about it.

Facilitator: Yeah. The thing that's going to be hardest is to stay out of the shell.

Art: (Still crying) Well, yeah, if I can keep talking about it I can come out and stay out, but I'm gonna have to, y' know, protect me. It hurts. It's actually hurting to talk about it.

One can see very clearly here the deeper acceptance of this withdrawn self as being himself. But the beginning of change is equally evident.

Still another person reporting shortly after his workshop experience says, 'I came away from the workshop feeling much more deeply that "It's all right to be me with all my strengths and weaknesses." My wife told me that I seem more authentic, more real, more genuine.'

This feeling of greater realness and authenticity is a very common experience. It would appear that the individual is learning to accept and *be* himself and is thus laying the foundation for change. He is closer to his own feelings, hence they are no longer so rigidly organized and are more open to change.

One woman writes to tell how her father died very shortly after the encounter group, and she made a long and difficult trip to join her mother. '... a trip that seemed interminable with its confusing connections, my own bewilderment and deep sorrow, lack of sleep, and serious concern over mother's ill-health in the future. All I knew through the five days I spent there was that I wanted to *be* just the way I felt – that I wanted no "anaesthetic", no conventional screen between myself and my feelings, and that the only way I could achieve this was by fully accepting the experience, by *yielding* to shock and grief. This feeling of accepting and yielding has remained with me ever since. Quite frankly, I think the workshop had a great deal to do with my willingness to accept this experience.'

9. *The cracking of façades*. As the sessions continue, so many things tend to occur together that it is hard to know which to describe first. It should again be stressed that these different threads and stages interweave and overlap. One of the

threads is the increasing impatience with defences. As time goes on the group finds it unbearable that any member should live behind a mask or front. The polite words, the intellectual understanding of each other and of relationships, the smooth coin of tact and cover-up – amply satisfactory for interactions outside – are just not good enough. The expression of self by some members of the group has made it very clear that a deeper and more basic encounter is *possible*, and the group appears to strive intuitively and unconsciously towards this goal. Gently at times, almost savagely at others, the group *demands* that the individual be himself, that his current feelings not be hidden, that he remove the mask of ordinary social intercourse. In one group there was a highly intelligent and quite academic man who had been rather perceptive in his understanding of others but revealed himself not at all. The attitude of the group was finally expressed sharply by one member when he said, 'Come out from behind that lectern, Doc. Stop giving us speeches. Take off your dark glasses. We want to know *you*.'

In Synanon, the fascinating group so successfully involved in making persons out of drug addicts, this ripping away of façades is often dramatic. An excerpt from one of the 'synanons' or group sessions makes this clear:

Joe: (Speaking to Gina) I wonder when you're going to stop sounding so good in synanons. Every synanon that I'm in with you, someone asks you a question and you've got a beautiful book written. All made out about what went down and how you were wrong and how you realized you were wrong and all that kind of bullshit. When are you going to stop doing that? How do you feel about Art?

Gina: I have nothing against Art.

Will: You're a nut. Art hasn't got any damn sense. He's been in there, yelling at you and Moe, and you've got everything so cool.

Gina: No, I feel he's very insecure in a lot of ways but that has nothing to do with me . . .

Joe: You act like you're so goddam understanding.

Gina: I was *told* to act as if I understand.

Joe: Well, you're in a synanon now. You're not supposed to be acting like you're such a goddamn healthy person. Are you so well?

Gina: No.

Joe: Well, why the hell don't you quit acting as if you were?[6]

If I am indicating that the group is quite violent at times in tearing down a façade or defence, this is accurate. On the other hand, it can also be sensitive and gentle. The man who was accused of hiding behind a lectern was deeply hurt by this attack, and over the lunch-hour looked very troubled, as though he might break into tears at any moment. When the group reconvened, the members sensed this and treated him very gently, enabling him to tell us his own tragic personal story, which accounted for his aloofness and his intellectual and academic approach to life.

10. *The individual receives feedback.* In the process of this freely expressive interaction, the individual rapidly acquires a great deal of data as to how he appears to others. The hail-fellow-well-met finds that others resent his exaggerated friendliness. The executive who weighs his words carefully and speaks with heavy precision may discover for the first time that others regard him as stuffy. A woman who shows a somewhat excessive desire to be of help to others is told in no uncertain terms that some group members do not want her for a mother. All this can be decidedly upsetting, but so long as these various bits of information are fed back in the context of caring which is developing in the group, they seem highly constructive.

An example of one kind of feedback occurred in a group where it was suggested that members describe each other as animate or inanimate objects. This gave some powerful feedback.

John: (To Alma) As long as we're talking about things, might as well pick on you a little bit. You remind me of a butterfly. (Laughter.)

6. D. Casriel, *So Fair a House* (Englewood Cliffs, N.J.: Prentice-Hall, 1963), p. 81.

Alma: Why is that? I mean how, I mean, why do you say a butterfly?

John: Well, to me a butterfly is a curious thing. It's a thing you can get up pretty close to, as you might say, as a new friend, but just about the time that you can get up to it and pet it or bring it in closer to you and look at it, it flits away.

Alma: (laughs nervously.)

John: Y' know, it's gone, and until you wear it out, you know or wet it down until it's so tired it can't fly any more – or you teach it to trust you – you can't get close enough to it to touch it or find out anything real about it, except from a distance. You remind me of a butterfly in that way. Something that possibly would be quite pretty to look at close up, but you can never get that close.

To tell a woman that she is fearful of any close relationship is something which would occur very rarely indeed in ordinary social interaction. But such data are often made available to the person in an encounter group.

Feedback can at times be very warm and positive, as the following recorded excerpt indicates:

Leo: (Very softly and gently) I've been struck with this ever since she talked about her waking in the night, that she has a very delicate sensitivity. (Turning to Mary and speaking almost caressingly) And somehow I perceive – even looking at you or in your eyes – a very – almost like a gentle touch and from this gentle touch you can tell many – things – you sense in – this manner.

Fred: Leo, when you said that, that she has this kind of delicate sensitivity, I just felt, *Lord yes!* Look at her eyes.

Leo: M—h'm.

A much more extended instance of both negative and positive feedback, triggering a significant new experience of self-understanding and encounter with the group, is taken from the diary kept by a young man who felt very much unloved. He had been telling the group that he had no feeling for them and felt they had no feeling for him.

. . . Then, a girl lost patience with me and said she didn't feel she could give any more. She said I looked like a bottomless well, and she wondered how many times I had to be told that I *was* cared for. By this time I was feeling panicky, and I was saying to myself, 'God, can it be true that I can't be satisfied and that I'm somehow compelled to pester people for attention until I drive them away!'

At this point while I was really worried, a nun in the group spoke up. She said that I had not alienated her with some negative things I had said to her. She said she liked me, and she couldn't understand why I couldn't see that. She said she felt concerned for me and wanted to help me. With that, something began to really dawn on me and I voiced it somewhat like the following. 'You mean you are still sitting there feeling for me what I say I want you to feel and that somewhere down inside me I'm stopping it from touching me?' I relaxed appreciably and began really to wonder why I had shut their caring out so much. I couldn't find the answer, and one woman said: 'It looks like you are trying to stay continuously as deep in your feelings as you were this afternoon. It would make sense to me for you to draw back and assimilate it. Maybe if you don't push so hard, you can rest a while and then move back into your feelings more naturally.'

Her making the last suggestion really took effect. I saw the sense in it, and almost immediately I settled back very relaxed with something of a feeling of a bright, warm day dawning inside me. In addition to taking the pressure off of myself, I was for the first time really warmed by the friendly feelings which I felt they had for me. It is difficult to say why I felt liked only just then, but as opposed to the earlier sessions I really *believed* they cared for me. I never have fully understood why I stood their affection off for so long, but at that point I almost abruptly began to trust that they did care. The measure of the effectiveness of this change lies in what I said next. I said, 'Well, that really takes care of me. I'm really ready to listen to someone else now.' I *meant* that, too.[7]

11. *Confrontation.* There are times when the term feedback is far too mild to describe the interactions that take place — when it is better said that one individual *confronts* another, directly 'levelling' with him. Such confrontations can be positive, but frequently they are decidedly negative, as the following example will make abundantly clear. In one of the last

7. G. F. Hall, 'A Participant's Experience in a Basic Encounter Group.' Unpublished manuscript, 1965. Mimeographed.

sessions of a group, Alice had made some quite vulgar and contemptuous remarks to John, who was entering religious work. The next morning, Norma, who has been a very quiet person in the group, takes the floor:

Norma (loud sigh): Well, I don't have *any* respect for you, Alice. *None!* (Pause.) There's about a hundred things going through my mind I want to say to you, and *by God* I hope I get through 'em all! First of all, if you wanted us to respect you, then why couldn't you respect *John's* feelings last night? *Why have you been on him today?* H'mm? Last night — *couldn't you — couldn't you* accept — *couldn't you* comprehend in any way at all that — that *he felt* his unworthiness in the service of God? *Couldn't you accept this* or did you have to dig into it today to find something *else* there? H'mm? I personally don't think John has any problems that are *any of your damn business!* ... Any real woman that I know wouldn't have acted as you have this week, and particularly what you said this afternoon. That was so *crass!!* It just made me want to puke, right there!!! And — I'm just *shaking* I'm so mad at you — I don't think you've been real once this week! ... I'm so infuriated that I *want to come over and beat the hell out of you!! I want to slap you across the mouth so hard and* — oh, and you're so, you're many years above me — and I respect age, and I respect people who are older than me, *but I don't respect you, Alice. At all!* (A startled pause.)

It may relieve the reader to know that these two women came to accept each other, not completely but much more understandingly, before the end of the session. But this *was* a confrontation!

12. *The helping relationship outside the group sessions.* No account of the group process would be adequate, in my opinion, if it did not mention many ways in which group members assist each other. One of the exciting aspects of any group experience is the way in which, when an individual is struggling to express himself, or wrestling with a personal problem, or hurting because of some painful new discovery about himself, other

members give him help. This may be within the group, as mentioned earlier, but occurs even more frequently in contacts outside the group. When I see two individuals going for a walk together, or conversing in a quiet corner, or hear that they stayed up talking until 3 A.M. I feel it is quite probable that at some later time in the group we will hear that one was gaining strength and help from the other, that the second person was making available his understanding, his support, his experience, his caring – making himself *available* to the other. An incredible gift of healing is possessed by many persons, if only they feel freed to give it, and experience in an encounter group seems to make this possible.

Let me offer an example of the healing effect of the attitudes of group members both outside and within the group meetings. This is taken from a letter written by a workshop member to the group one month later. He speaks of the difficulties and depressing circumstances he has met during that month and adds:

I have come to the conclusion that my experiences with you have profoundly affected me. I am truly grateful. This is different than personal therapy. None of you *had* to care about me. None of you had to seek me out and let me know of things you thought would help me. None of you had to let me know I was of help to you. Yet you did, and as a result it has far more meaning than anything I have so far experienced. When I feel the need to hold back and not live spontaneously, for whatever reasons, I remember that twelve persons just like those before me now said to let go and be congruent, be myself and of all unbelievable things they even loved me more for it. This has given me the *courage* to come out of myself many times since then. Often it seems my very doing of this helps the others to experience similar freedom.

13. *The basic encounter*. Running through some of the trends I have just been describing is the fact that individuals come into much closer and more direct contact with each other than is customary in ordinary life. This appears to be one of the most central, intense, and change-producing aspects of group experience. To illustrate, I should like to draw an example from a recent workshop group. A man tells through his tears of the tragic loss of his child, a grief which he is experiencing

fully for the first time, not holding back his feelings in any way. Another says to him, also with tears in his eyes, 'I've never before felt a real physical hurt in me from the pain of another. I feel completely with you.' This is a basic encounter.

From another group, a mother with several children who describes herself as 'a loud, prickly, hyperactive individual', whose marriage has been on the rocks and who has felt that life was just not worth living, writes:

I had really buried under a layer of concrete many feelings I was afraid people were going to laugh at or stomp on which, needless to say, was working all kinds of hell on my family and on me. I had been looking forward to the workshop with my last few crumbs of hope. It was really a needle of trust in a huge haystack of despair [She tells of some of her experiences in the group, and adds] . . . the real turning point for me was a simple gesture on your part of putting your arm around my shoulder one afternoon when I had made some crack about you not being a member of the group – that no one could cry on your shoulder. In my notes I had written the night before, 'There is no man in the world who loves me!' You seemed so genuinely concerned that day that I was overwhelmed . . . I *received* the gesture as one of the first feelings of acceptance – of me, just the dumb way I am, prickles and all – that I had ever experienced. I have felt needed, loving, competent, furious, frantic, anything and everything but just plain *loved*. You can imagine the flood of gratitude, humility, release that swept over me. I wrote with considerable joy, '*I* actually felt *loved*.' I doubt that I shall soon forget it.

Such I-Thou relationships (to use Buber's term again) occur with some frequency in these group sessions and nearly always bring a moistness to the eyes of the participants.

One member, trying to sort out his experiences immediately after a workshop, speaks of the 'commitment to relationship' which often developed on the part of two individuals – not necessarily individuals who have liked each other initially – he goes on to say, '. . .the incredible fact experienced over and over by members of the group was that, when a negative feeling was fully expressed to another, the relationship grew and the negative feeling was replaced by a deep acceptance for the other . . . Thus real change seemed to occur when feelings were experienced and expressed in the context of the relationship. "I can't *stand* the way you talk!" turned into a real under-standing and affection for you the *way* you talk.' This statement seems to capture some of the more complex meanings of the term basic encounter.

14. *The expression of positive feelings and closeness.* As indicated in the last section, an inevitable part of the group process seems to be that when feelings are expressed and can be accepted in a relationship, then a great deal of closeness and positive feeling results. Thus, as the sessions proceed, an increasing feeling of warmth and group spirit and trust is built up, not out of positive attitudes only but out of a realness which includes both positive and negative feeling. One member tried to capture this in writing shortly after a workshop by saying that if he were trying to sum it up, '. . . it would have to do with what I call confirmation – a kind of confirmation of myself, of the uniqueness and universal qualities of men, a confirmation that when we can be human together something positive can emerge.'

A particularly poignant expression of these positive attitudes was shown in the group where Norma confronted Alice with her bitterly angry feelings. Joan, the facilitator, was deeply upset and began to weep. The positive and healing attitudes of the group for their own *leader* is an unusual example of the closeness and personal quality of the relationships.

Joan (crying): I somehow feel that it's so *damned* easy for me to – to put myself *inside* of another person and I just guess I can feel that – for John and Alice and for you, Norma.

Alice: And it's *you* that's hurt.

Joan: Maybe I am taking some of that hurt. I guess I am (crying).

Alice: That's a wonderful gift. I wish I had it.

Joan: You have a lot of it.

Peter: In a way you bear the – I guess in a special way, because you're the – facilitator, you've probably borne an extra heavy burden for all of us . . . we grope to try to accept one another as we are, and – for each of us in various ways I guess we reach things and we say, *please* accept me; I want to leave this *right here*, and . . .

Norma: Then we don't.

Peter: And – and we're placing this burden on you now, perhaps, and with your feelings it can be an extra heavy burden – for people asking you please to *accept me* this way. You think it might be that?

Joan (still weeping): Well, I really don't put the blame on the other people; I think that's – that's *my* problem, really, you know, that I *take* that burden, or whatever it is. I mean I'd take it just as much if I weren't the facilitator – I don't think it's the role.

Peter: No, no, it's not the role . . .

Norma: No, definitely not . . .

George: I don't think it's what people put on your mind; I think it's this fantastic sensitivity you have – what you share in – and then you bear the burden – I think you mean a lot more to me now than before. There were times when I wondered about you and whether you were going to approach us as people or as clients. I think I did say once this week, though, that I had the feeling that if it ever became necessary, you would show the skeleton in the closet – if you thought it were necessary. You're that *honest* about things. And I think that this shows that you – you *showed* it; the other side of you that we haven't seen all week. It makes me feel bad that I'm this way – one in the group that doesn't help you at the moment to feel better.

Some may be very critical of a 'leader' so involved and so sensitive that she weeps at the tensions in the group which she has taken into herself. For myself it is simply another evidence that when people are real with each other, they have an astonishing ability to heal a person with a real and understanding love, whether that person is 'participant' or 'leader'.

15. *Behaviour changes in the group.* It would seem from observation that many changes in behaviour occur in the group itself. Gestures change. The tone of voice changes, becoming sometimes stronger, sometimes softer, usually more spontaneous, less artificial, with more feeling. Individuals show an astonishing amount of thoughtfulness and helpfulness towards each other.

Our major concern, however, is with the behaviour changes that occur following the group experience. This constitutes the most significant question, on which we need much more study and research. One person gives a catalogue which may seem too pat, but which is echoed in many other statements, of the changes he sees in himself. 'I am more open, spontaneous. I express myself more freely. I am more sympathetic, empathic, and tolerant. I am more confident. I am more religious in my own way. My relations with my family, friends, and co-workers are more honest and I express my likes and dislikes and true feelings more openly. I admit ignorance more readily. I am more cheerful. I want to help others more.'

Another says, '. . . Since the workshop there has been found a new relationship with my parents. It has been trying and hard. However, I have found a greater freedom in talking with them, especially my father. Steps have been made towards being closer to my mother than I have ever been in the last five years.' Another says, 'It helped clarify my feelings about my work, gave me more enthusiasm for it, made me more honest and cheerful with my co-workers and also more open when I was hostile. It made my relationship with my wife more open, deeper. We felt freer to talk about anything and we felt confident that anything we talked about we could work through.'

Sometimes the changes described are very subtle. 'The primary change is the more positive view of my ability to allow myself to *hear*, and to become involved with someone else's "silent scream".'

At the risk of making the outcomes sound too good, I will add one more statement written shortly after a workshop by a mother. She says, 'The immediate impact on my children was of interest to both me and my husband. I feel that having been so accepted and loved by a group of strangers was so supportive that when I returned home my love for the people closest to me was much more spontaneous. Also, the practice I had in accepting and loving others during the workshop was evident in my relationships with my close friends.'

In a later chapter I shall try to summarize the different kinds of behaviour changes we find, both positive and negative.

Thus far one might think that every aspect of the group process is positive. As far as the evidence at hand indicates, it appears that it is nearly always a positive process for a majority of the participants. Failures nevertheless result. Let me try to describe briefly some negative aspects of the group process as they sometimes occur.

The most obvious deficiency of the intensive group experience is that frequently the behaviour changes that occur, if any, are not lasting. This is often recognized by the participants. One says, 'I wish I had the ability to hold permanently the "openness" I left the conference with.' Another says, 'I experienced a lot of acceptance, warmth, and love at the workshop. I find it hard to carry the ability to share this in the same way with people outside the workshop. I find it easier to slip back into my old unemotional role than to do the work necessary to open relationships.'

Sometimes group members experience this phenomenon of 'relapse' quite philosophically. 'The group experience is not a way of life but a reference point. My images of our group, even though I am unsure of some of their meanings, give me a comforting and useful perspective on my normal routine. They are like a mountain which I have climbed and enjoyed and to which I hope occasionally to return.' I will comment further on this 'slippage' in the chapter on research findings.

A second potential risk involved in the intensive group experience, and one often mentioned in public discussion, is that the individual may become deeply involved in revealing himself and then be left with problems which are not worked through. There have been a number of reports of people who have felt, following an intensive group experience, that they must go to a therapist to work through the feelings which were opened up in the intensive experience of the workshop and were left unresolved. It is obvious that without knowing more about each individual situation it is difficult to say whether this is a negative outcome or a partially or entirely positive one. There are also very occasional accounts of an individual having a psychotic episode during or immediately following an intensive group experience. On the other side of the picture is the fact that individuals have also lived through what were clearly psychotic episodes, and lived through them very constructively, in the context of a basic encounter group. My own tentative clinical judgement would be that the more positively the group process proceeds the less likely it is that any individual would be psychologically damaged through membership in the group. It is obvious, however, that this is a serious issue and that much more needs to be known.

Some of the tension that exists in workshop members as a result of this potential for damage is well described by one participant when he says, 'I feel the workshop had some very precious moments for me when I felt very close indeed to particular persons. It had some frightening moments when its potency was very evident, and I realized a particular person might be deeply hurt or greatly helped, but I couldn't predict which.'

There is another risk or deficiency in the basic encounter group. Until very recent years it has been unusual for a workshop to include both husband and wife. This can be a real problem if significant change has taken place in one spouse during or as a result of the workshop experience. One individual feels this risk clearly after attending a workshop. He says, 'I think there is a great danger to a marriage when only one spouse attends a group. It is too hard for the other spouse to compete with the group individually and collectively.' One of the frequent after-effects of the intensive group experience is that it brings out into the open for discussion marital tensions which have been kept under cover.

Another risk which has sometimes been a cause of real concern in mixed intensive workshops is that very positive and warm and loving feelings can develop between members of the encounter group (as is evident both in some of the foregoing examples and in later chapters). Inevitably some of these feelings have a sexual component, and this can be a matter of great concern to the participants and a profound threat to their spouses if these are not worked through satisfactorily in the workshop. Also the close and loving feelings which develop may become a source of threat and marital difficulty when a wife, for example, has not been present, but projects many fears about the loss of her spouse – whether well-founded or not – onto the workshop experience.

A man who had been in a mixed group of men and women executives wrote to me a year later and mentioned the strain in his marriage that resulted from his association with Marge, a member of his basic encounter group. 'There was a problem about Marge. There had occurred a very warm feeling on my part for Marge, a great compassion, for I felt she was *very* lonely. I believe the warmth was sincerely reciprocal. At any rate she wrote me a long affectionate letter, which I let my wife read. I was *proud* that Marge could feel that way about me' (for he had felt very worthless). 'But my wife was alarmed, because she read a love affair into the words – at least a *potential* threat. I stopped writing to Marge because I felt rather clandestine after that. My wife has since participated in an "encounter group" herself, and she now understands. I have resumed writing to Marge.' Obviously, not all such episodes would have such a harmonious ending.

It is of interest in this connection that there has been increasing experimentation in recent years with 'couples workshops' and with workshops for industrial executives and their spouses.

Perhaps one other episode of 'falling in love' in the group will be meaningful because it is reported with such utter frankness by Emma, a participant, a divorcee with children.

. . . Early in the first week I became aware of one man in the group who seemed to be confident about his masculinity, yet warm, insightful, and kind. This combination attracted me, and I recognized that this was the kind of male figure that gives me peace. By Thursday of the first week we had begun to find many things in common and spent time under the pines together. On Thursday, after the 'T' group, he said to me, 'Emma, I think I see that you may have threatened your husband and I think I see that you may threaten men.' In answer to my unspoken query, he said, 'You are so damn sure that you are right when you get an insight.' This sent my self-esteem into my shoes as we walked into the general session and he sat down beside me. About five minutes later he turned to me with tears in his eyes and said, 'My God, Emma, what I saw in you is what I stub my toe on in my own personnel work in the laboratories every day I work.' As he made this remark, I fell in love with him from the top of my head to the tip of my toes. By making the problem a common one to males and females, I was freed from the box labelled 'You are Destructive to Men'.

Saturday noon Allen went home to his family and I remained in a state of wedding throughout Saturday and Sunday. Sunday night when he returned I perceived him as flooding me with love from his eyes and my world was complete. Monday morning very early I awakened sobbing. I was a little girl with a short ruffled dress. A hazy male figure hovered on the fringe of the scene. For the next three hours I experienced what it felt like to be loved by a father. It was interesting that in the three hours of feeling such a love, I never lost the feeling of being a woman in love with a man. Somehow the quality of Allen's love seemed to permit the feeling of father-love in proper time and space as an enhancement to the feeling of mating. I'm afraid I am not making myself very clear but it is the best I can do . . .

. . . Friday morning, on our last day, Allen insisted after the 'T' group that we have a few minutes together. We sat on a low rock wall in the sunshine. He asked me if I would talk about our two weeks. What I said in reply was something like this: 'We have found our way along an obstacle course. The relationship has been delicate and fragile. Once I put my trust in you I never lost faith that you could find the way. Of the future? I do not think I will fantasy you as my husband. I think I will always honor and love you as Allen E. who, by the quality of his love, has built into me the capacity to be a lovable and loving woman. I trust that in some way this experience has given you greater awareness of your capacity to be a loving man. What will sustain us in the future? It feels to me that the sustaining force will be that we both will know that as we interact with our separate families and professional colleagues, each in his own way will nurture. I have even some elusive feeling that my own three children in perceiving the new me will in some way come to know what it feels like to have a father.' When I finished, Allen who has much greater insight and facility to express it than I, with tearful eyes, commented: 'You have expressed it beautifully! We have lived a lifetime together.'

At home this week one fear box after another keeps crumbling away as the new me oozes out. As I feel my new world, a serenity is so pervasive that it seems pudding-like and touchable . . .

Here is a mature handling of a deep and delicate love relationship. I cannot doubt that it made for further growth and development in each of these individuals.

One more negative potential growing out of encounter groups has become evident in recent years. Some individuals who have participated in previous encounter groups may exert a stultifying influence on new workshops they attend. They sometimes exhibit what I think of as the 'old pro' phenomenon. They feel they have learned the 'rules of the game', and subtly or openly try to impose these rules on newcomers. Thus, instead of promoting true expressiveness or spontaneity, they endeavour to substitute new rules for old – to make members feel guilty if they are not expressing feelings, or are reluctant to voice criticism or hostility, or are talking about situations outside the group relationship, or are fearful to reveal themselves. These 'old pros' seem to attempt to substitute a new tyranny in interpersonal relationships in the place of older conventional restrictions. To me this is a perversion of the true group process. We need to ask ourselves how this travesty on spontaneity comes about. Personally, I wonder about the quality of the facilitation in their previous group experiences.

CONCLUSION

I have tried to give a naturalistic, observational picture of some of the common elements of the process which occur in the climate of freedom of an encounter group. I have pointed out some of the risks and shortcomings of the group experience. I hope I have also made clear that this is an area in which an enormous amount of deeply perceptive study and research is needed.

3

Can I Be a Facilitative Person in a Group?

When I finished the chapter on the process of encounter groups, I thought the next step – and a very logical one – would be to write on 'The Facilitation of Encounter Groups'. But it simply would not jell in my mind, and I delayed for more than a year. I kept thinking of all the very different styles of leaders I have known and with whom I have co-led groups. Any such chapter by its very brevity would have to be so homogenized that every truth in it would also be to some extent a falsehood.

Then I narrowed my sights and thought I would write on 'My Way of Facilitating a Group', hoping to stimulate others to do the same. But in a discussion with various other facilitators, many of them members of our staff – a discussion which has enriched this whole presentation – I was challenged on this topic too. I came to see that it still had the flavour of expertise in it, which I do not want to emphasize. I think the present title catches my real purpose. I want to write as openly as I am able about my efforts to be a facilitative person in a group, express what I can of my strengths, weaknesses, and uncertainties as I try to engage effectively in the honest artistry of interpersonal relations.

Background of Philosophy and Attitudes

One does not enter a group as a *tabula rasa*. So I would like to state some of the attitudes and convictions I bring with me.

I trust the group, given a reasonably facilitating climate, to develop its own potential and that of its members. For me, this capacity of the group is an awesome thing. Perhaps as a corollary of this, I have gradually developed a great deal of trust in the group process. This is undoubtedly similar to the trust I came to have in the process of therapy in the individual, when it was facilitated rather than directed. To me the group seems like an organism, having a sense of its own direction even though it could not define that direction intellectually. This is reminiscent of a medical motion picture which once made a deep impression on me. It was a photo-micrographic film showing the white blood corpuscles moving very randomly through the blood stream, until a disease bacterium appeared. Then, in a fashion which could only be described as purposeful, they moved towards it. They surrounded it and gradually engulfed and destroyed it, then moved on again in their random way. Similarly, it seems to me, a group recognizes unhealthy elements in its process, focuses on them, clears them up or eliminates them, and moves on towards becoming a healthier group. This is my way of saying that I have seen the 'wisdom of the organism' exhibited at every level from cell to group.

This is not to say that every group is 'successful'[1] or that the process is always identical. One group may start at a very rapid, inexpressive level and move a few small steps towards greater freedom. Another may start at a very spontaneous, feelingful level and move a long way towards developing their potential to the fullest. Both of these movements seem to me part of the group process, and I trust each group equally, though my personal enjoyment of the two may be quite different.

Another attitude has to do with aims. I usually have no specific goal for a particular group and sincerely want it to develop its own directions. There are times when, because of some personal bias or anxiety, I *have* had a specific goal for a group. When this has happened, either the group has carefully defeated that aim or has spent enough time dealing with me so that I have truly regretted having a specific goal in mind. I

---

1. What is 'successful'? For the present I will settle for the simple sort of definition. If, a month after the group is over, a number of the participants feel that it was a meaningless, dissatisfying experience, or a hurtful one from which they are still recovering, then for them this was certainly not a successful group. If, on the other hand, most or all of the members still feel that it was a rewarding experience which somehow moved them forward in their own growth, then for me it deserves the label of a successful group.

stress the negative aspects of *specific* goals because, at the same time as I hope to avoid them, I also hope there will be some sort of process movement in the group, and even think I can predict some of the probable generalized directions, though not any specific direction. For me this is an important difference. The group will *move* – of this I am confident – but it would be presumptuous to think that I can or should *direct* that movement towards a *specific* goal.

In no basic philosophical way, so far as I can see, does this approach differ from that which I have adopted for years in individual therapy. However, my behaviour is often quite different in a group from what it used to be in a one-to-one relationship. I attribute this to the personal growth experienced in groups.

Ordinarily the question of how my style of facilitation looks to another person is not important to me. In that sense I usually feel reasonably competent and comfortable. On the other hand, I know from experience that I can be at least temporarily jealous of a co-leader who seems more facilitative than myself.

My hope is gradually to become as much a participant in the group as a facilitator. This is difficult to describe without making it appear that I am consciously playing two different roles. If you watch a group member who is honestly being himself, you will see that at times he expresses feelings, attitudes, and thoughts primarily directed towards facilitating the growth of another member. At other times, with equal genuineness, he will express feelings or concerns which have as their obvious goal the opening of himself to the risk of more growth. This describes me too, except that I know I am likely to be the second, or risking, kind of person more often in the later than in the earlier phases of the group. Each facet is a real part of me, not a role.

Perhaps another brief analogy will be useful here. If I am trying to explain some scientific phenomenon to a five-year-old, my terminology and even attitude will be very different from those I display if I am explaining the same thing to a bright sixteen-year-old. Does this mean that I am playing two roles? Of course not – it simply means that two facets or expressions of the real me have been brought into play. In the same way, in one moment I really want to be facilitative towards some person, and in another, to risk exposing some new aspect of myself.

I believe that the way I serve as facilitator has significance in the life of the group, but that the group process is much more important than my statements or behaviour, and will take place if I do not get in the way of it. I certainly feel responsible *to* the participants, but not *for* them.

In any group to some degree, but especially in a so-called academic course I am conducting in encounter group fashion, I want very much to have the *whole* person present, in both his affective and cognitive modes. I have not found this easy to achieve since most of us seem to choose one mode rather than the other at any given instant. Yet this still remains a way of being which has much value for me. I try to make progress in myself, and in groups I facilitate, in permitting the whole person, with his ideas as well as his feelings – with feelings permeated with ideas and ideas permeated with feelings – to be fully present. In a recent seminar, for reasons I do not fully understand, this was achieved by all of us to a most gratifying degree.

Climate-Setting Function

I tend to open a group in an extremely unstructured way, perhaps with no more than a simple comment: 'I suspect we will know each other a great deal better at the end of these group sessions than we do now,' or 'Here we are. We can make of this group experience exactly what we wish,' or 'I'm a little uneasy, but I feel somewhat reassured when I look around at you and realize we're all in the same boat. Where do we start?' In a recorded discussion with a group of other facilitators I stated this view as follows.

Partly because I do trust the group, I can usually be quite loose and relaxed in a group even from the first. That's overstating it somewhat, for I always feel a little anxiety when a group starts, but by and large I feel, 'I don't have any idea what's going to happen, but I think what's going to happen will be all right,' and I think I tend to communicate nonverbally 'Well none of us seem to know what's going to happen, but it doesn't seem to be something to worry about.' I believe that my relaxation and lack of any desire to guide may have a freeing influence on others.

I listen as carefully, accurately, and sensitively as I am able, to each individual who expresses himself. Whether the utterance is superficial or significant, I *listen*. To me the individual who speaks is worthwhile, worth understanding; consequently *he* is worthwhile for having expressed something. Colleagues say that in this sense I 'validate' the person.

There is no doubt that I am selective in my listening, hence 'directive' if people wish to accuse me of this. I am centred in the group member who is speaking, and am unquestionably much less interested in the details of his quarrel with his wife, or of his difficulties on the job, or his disagreement with what has just been said, than in the *meaning* these experiences have for him now and the *feelings* they arouse in him. It is to these meanings and feelings that I try to respond.

I wish very much to make the climate psychologically safe for the individual. I want him to feel from the first that if he risks saying something highly personal, or absurd, or hostile, or cynical, there will be at least one person in the circle who respects him enough to hear him clearly and listen to that statement as an authentic expression of himself.

There is a slightly different way in which I also want to make the climate safe for the member. I am well aware that one cannot make the experience safe from the pain of new insight or growth, or the pain of honest feedback from others. However, I would like the individual to feel that whatever happens *to* him or *within* him, I will be psychologically very much *with* him in moments of pain or joy, or the combination of the two which is such a frequent mark of growth. I think I can usually sense when a participant is frightened or hurting, and it is at those moments that I give him some sign, verbal or nonverbal, that I perceive this and am a companion to him as he lives in that hurt or fear.

The Acceptance of the Group

I have a great deal of patience with a group and with the individual within it. If there is one thing I have learned and relearned in recent years, it is that it is ultimately very rewarding to accept the group exactly where it *is*. If a group wishes to intellectualize, or discuss quite superficial problems, or is emotionally very closed, or very frightened of personal communication, these tendencies rarely 'bug' me as much as they do some other leaders. I am well aware that certain exercises, tasks set up by the facilitator, can practically force the group to more of a here-and-now communication or more of a feelings level. There are leaders who do these things very skilfully, and with good effect at the time. However, I am enough of a scientist-clinician to make many casual follow-up inquiries, and I know that frequently the lasting result of such procedures is not nearly as satisfying as the immediate effect. At its best it may lead to discipleship (which I happen not to like): 'What a marvellous leader he is to have *made* me open up when I had no intention of doing it!' It can also lead to a rejection of the whole experience. 'Why did I do those silly things he asked me to?' At worst, it can make the person feel that his private self has been in some way violated, and he will be careful never to expose himself to a group again. From my experience I know that if I attempt to push a group to a deeper level it is not, in the long run, going to work.

So for me, I have found that it pays off to live with the group exactly where it is. Thus I have worked with a cluster of very inhibited top-notch scientists – mostly in the physical sciences – where feelings were rarely expressed openly and personal encounter at a deep level was simply not seen. Yet this group became much more free, expressive, and innovative, and showed many positive results of our meetings.

I have worked with high-level educational administrators – probably the most rigid and well-defended group in our culture – with similar results. This is not to say it is always easy for me. In one particular group of educators there had been much superficial and intellectual talk, but gradually they moved to a deeper level. Then in an evening session the talk became more and more trivial. One person asked, 'Are we doing what we *want* to do?' And the answer was an almost unanimous. 'No'. But within moments the talk again became social chatter about matters in which I had no interest. I was in a quandary. In order to allay a considerable early anxiety in the group, I had stressed in the first session that they could make of it exactly what they wished, and operationally they seemed to be saying very loudly, 'We want to spend expensive, hard-won week-end time talking of trivia.' To express my feelings of boredom and annoyance seemed contradictory to the freedom I had given them.[2] After wrestling within myself for a few moments, I decided that they had a perfect right to talk trivia, and I had a perfect right not to endure it. So I walked quietly out of the room and went to bed. After I left, and the next morning, the reactions were as varied as the participants. One felt rebuked and punished, another felt I had played a trick on them, a third felt ashamed of their time-wasting, others felt as disgusted as I at their trival interchanges. I told them that, to the best of my awareness, I was simply trying to make my behaviour match my contradictory feelings, but that they were entitled to their own perceptions. At any rate, after that the interactions were far more meaningful.

Acceptance of the Individual

I am willing for the participant to commit or not to commit himself to the group. If a person wishes to remain psychologically on the sidelines, he has my implicit permission to do so. The group itself may or may not be willing for him to remain in this stance but personally I am willing. One sceptical college administrator said that the main thing he had learned was that he could withdraw from personal participation, be comfortable about it, and realize that he would not be coerced. To me, this seemed a valuable learning and one which would

2. Had I said in the first meeting, '*We* can make of this what we wish,' which would have been preferable and probably more honest, I would have felt free to say, 'I don't like what we are making of it.' But I was quite certain that in my attempt at reassurance I had said, 'You can make of it what you wish.' We always pay for our blunders.

make it much more possible for him actually to participate at the next opportunity. Recent reports on his behaviour, a full year later, suggest that he gained and changed from his seeming non-participation.

Silence or muteness in the individual are acceptable to me providing I am quite certain it is not unexpressed pain or resistance.

I tend to accept statements at their face value. As a facilitator (as in my function as therapist) I definitely prefer to be a gullible person; I will believe that you are telling me the way it is in you. If not, you are entirely free to correct your message at a later point, and are likely to do so. I do not want to waste my time being suspicious, or wondering, 'What does he *really* mean?'

I respond *more* to present feelings than to statements about past experiences but am willing for both to be present in the communication. I do not like the rule: 'We will only talk about the here and now.'

I try to make clear that whatever happens will happen from the choices of the group, whether these are clear and conscious, gropingly uncertain, or unconscious. As I become increasingly a member of the group, I willingly carry my share of *influence*, but do not *control* what happens.

I am usually able to feel comfortable with the fact that in eight hours we can accomplish eight hours' worth and in forty hours we can accomplish forty hours' worth – while in a one-hour demonstration session we can accomplish one hour's worth.

Empathic Understanding

My attempt to understand the exact meaning of what the person is communicating is the most important and most frequent of my behaviours in a group.

For me, it is a part of this understanding that I try to delve through complications and get the communication back on to the track of the *meaning* that it has to the *person*. For example, after a very complicated and somewhat incoherent statement by a husband I respond, 'And so, little by little, you have come to hold back things that previously you would have communicated to your wife? Is that it?'

'Yes.'

Feedback

I believe this is facilitative, since it clarifies the message for the speaker and helps the group members to understand and not waste time asking questions about or responding to the complicated details he has presented.

When talk is generalized or intellectualizing, I tend to select the self-referent meanings to respond to out of the total context. Thus I might say, 'Though you are speaking of all this in general terms of what everybody does in certain situations, I suspect you are speaking very much for yourself in saying that. Is that right?' Or, 'You say we all do and feel thus and so. Do you mean that *you* do and feel these things?'

At the beginning of one group, Al said some rather meaningful things, John, another member, started questioning and questioning him about what he had said, but I heard more than questions. I finally said to John, 'OK, you keep trying to get at what he said and what he meant, but I think you're trying to say something *to* him and I'm not sure what that is.' John thought for a moment and then began to speak for *himself*. Up to that moment, he had apparently been trying to get Al to articulate his (John's) feelings for him, so that he wouldn't have to voice them as coming from himself. This seems quite a common pattern.

I very much want my understanding to extend to both sides of a difference in feeling which is being expressed. Thus, in one group which was discussing marriage, two people held very different views. I responded, 'This is a real difference between the two of you, because you, Jerry, are saying "I like smoothness in a relationship. I like it to be nice and tranquil," and Winnie is saying, "To hell with that! I like communication." ' This helps to sharpen and clarify the significance of differences.

Operating in Terms of My Feelings

I have learned to be more and more free in making use of my own feelings as they exist in the moment, whether in relation to the group as a whole, or to one individual, or to myself. I nearly always feel a genuine and present concern for each member and for the group as a whole. It is hard to give any reason for this. It is just a fact. I value each person; but this valuing carries no guarantee of a permanent relationship. It is a concern and feeling which exists *now*. I think I feel it more clearly because I am not saying it is or will be permanent.

I believe I am quite sensitive to moments when an individual is feeling a readiness to speak or is close to pain or tears or anger. Thus one might say, 'Let's give Carlene a chance,' or 'You look as though you are really troubled about something. Do you want to let us in on it?'

It is probably particularly to hurt that I respond with empathic understanding. This desire to understand, and to stand psychologically with the person in pain, probably grows in part out of my therapeutic experience.

I endeavour to voice any *persisting* feelings which I am experiencing towards an individual or towards the group, in any significant or continuing relationship. Obviously such expressions will not come at the very beginning, since feelings are not yet persistent ones. I might, for example, take a dislike to someone's behaviour during the first ten minutes the group is together, but would be unlikely to voice it at that time. If the feeling persists, however, I would express it.

In discussing this point, one facilitator said, 'I've been trying to follow an eleventh commandment, "You shall always express the feelings you are experiencing."' Another discussant came back, 'You know how I react to that? That we should always have the *choice*. Sometimes I choose to express my feelings; other times I choose not to.'

I find myself much more in agreement with the second statement. If one can only be *aware* of all the complexity of my feelings in any given moment — if one is listening to oneself adequately — then it is possible to *choose* to express attitudes which are strong and persistent, or not to express them at this time if that seems highly inappropriate.

I *trust* the feelings, words, impulses, fantasies, that emerge in me. In this way I am using more than my conscious self, drawing on some of the capacities of my whole organism. For example, 'I suddenly had the fantasy that you are a princess, and that you would love it if we were all your subjects.' Or, 'I sense that you are the judge as well as the accused, and that you are saying sternly to yourself, "You are *guilty* on every count." '

Or the intuition may be a bit more complex. While a responsible business executive is speaking, I may suddenly have the fantasy of the small boy he is carrying around within himself – the small boy that he was, shy, inadequate, fearful – a child he endeavours to deny, of whom he is ashamed. And I am wishing that he would love and cherish this youngster. So I may voice this fantasy – not as something true, but as a fantasy in me. Often this brings a surprising depth of reaction and profound insights.

I want to be as expressive of positive and loving feelings as of negative or frustrated or angry ones. There may be a certain risk in this. In one instance I think I hurt the group process by being too expressive, early in the sessions, of warm feelings towards a number of members of the group. Because I was still perceived as the facilitator, this made it more difficult for others to bring out some of their negative and angry feelings, which were never voiced until the last session, bringing the group to a definitely unhappy ending.

I find it difficult to be easily or quickly aware of angry feelings in myself. I deplore this; am slowly learning in this respect.

It would be good to be unselfconsciously expressive of the feelings of the moment. There was one encounter group which was recorded – a group in which there was a great deal of movement. I did not hear the recordings until about two years later, and was amazed at some of the feelings I had expressed – towards others particularly. If a member of the group had said to me (after two years), 'You expressed this feeling towards me,' I'm sure I would have flatly denied it. Yet here was the evidence that, without weighing every word or thinking of possible consequences, I had, as a person in the group, unselfconsciously voiced whatever feeling I had in the moment. I felt good about this.

I seem to function best in a group when my 'owned' feelings – positive or negative – are in immediate interaction with those of a participant. To me this means that we are communicating on a deep level of personal meaning. It is the closest I get to an I-Thou relationship.

When asked a question, I try to consult my own feelings. If I sense it as being real and containing no other message than the question, then I will try my best to answer it. I feel no social compulsion, however, to answer simply because it is phrased as a question. There may be other messages in it far more important than the question itself.

A colleague has told me that I 'peel my own onion', that is express continuously deeper layers of feeling as I become aware of them in a group. I can only hope that this is true.

Confrontation and Feedback

I tend to confront individuals on specifics of their behaviour. 'I don't like the way you chatter on. Seems to me you give each message three or four times. I wish you would stop when you've completed your message.' 'To me you seem sort of like silly putty. Someone seems to reach you, to make a dent in you, but then it all springs back into place as though you hadn't been touched.'

And I like to confront another person only with feelings I am willing to claim as my own. These may at times be very strong. 'Never in my life have I been so pissed off at a group as I am at this one.' Or, to one man in the group, 'I woke up this morning feeling, "I never want to see you again." '

To attack a person's defences seems to me judgemental. If one says, 'You're hiding a lot of hostility,' or 'You are being highly intellectual, probably because you are afraid of your own feelings,' I believe such judgements and diagnoses are the opposite of facilitative. If, however, what I perceive as the person's coldness frustrates me or his intellectualizing irritates me, or his brutality to another person angers me, then I would like to face him with the frustration or the irritation or the anger that exists in *me*. To me this is *very* important.

Often in confronting someone I use quite specific material, given previously by the participant. 'Now you're being what you called the "poor lil ole country boy" once more.' 'Now it seems to me you are doing it again – the very thing you described – being the child who wants approval at any cost.'

If a person seems distressed by my confrontation or that of others, I am very willing to help him 'get off the hook' if he so desires. 'You look as though you have had about all you want to take. Would you like us to let you alone for the time being?' One can only be guided by the response, learning that sometimes he wants the feedback and confrontation to continue, even though it is painful for him.

Expression of Own Problems

If I am currently distressed by something in my own life, I am willing to express it in the group, but I do have some sort of professional conscience about this, for if I am paid to be a facilitator, then severe problems I feel I should work out in a staff group or with some therapist rather than taking group time. I am probably too cautious about this. In one instance – a slow-moving faculty group meeting once a week – I feel I really cheated them. At a certain point I was much upset about a personal problem, but felt that it did not concern the group and refrained from talking about it. As I look back, I think nothing would have more facilitated the group process than to articulate my upsetness; I believe it would have helped them to be more expressive.

If I do not feel free to express my personal problems, this has two unfortunate consequences. In the first place, I do not listen as well. In the second, I know from various experiences that the group is apt to perceive that I am upset and think *they* are at fault in some unknown way.

Avoidance of Planning and 'Exercises'

I try to avoid using any procedure that is *planned*; I have a real 'thing' about artificiality. If any planned procedure is tried, the group members should be as fully in on it as the facilitator, and should make the choice themselves as to whether they want to use that approach. On rare occasions, when frustrated or when a group has seemed to reach a plateau, I have tried what I think of as devices, but they rarely work. Probably this is because I myself lack faith that they are really useful.

It is possible to outline a procedure to group members, but what happens is up to them. In one apathetic group I suggested that we try to get out of our doldrums by doing as other groups had done: forming an inner circle and an outer one, with the person in the outer circle prepared to speak up for the real feelings of the individual in front of him. The group paid absolutely no attention to the suggestion and went on as though it had never been made. But within an hour, one man picked up the central aspect of this device and used it, saying, 'I want to speak for John and say what I believe he is *actually* feeling.' At least a dozen times in the next day or two, others used it – but in their own spontaneous way, not as a crude or stiff device.

To me nothing is a 'gimmick' if it occurs with real spontaneity. Thus, one may use role playing, bodily contact, psychodrama, exercises such as I have described, and various other procedures when they seem to express what one is actually feeling at the time.

This leads me to say that spontaneity is the most precious and elusive element I know. I do something very spontaneously, and it is highly effective. Then in the next group I may be strongly tempted to do it again – 'spontaneously' – and I have some difficulty in understanding why it falls flat. Obviously it has not been truly spontaneous.

Avoidance of Interpretive or Process Comments

I make comments on the group process very sparingly. They are apt to make the group self-conscious; they slow it down, giving members the sense that they are under scrutiny. Such comments also imply that I am not seeing them as persons but as sort of a lump or conglomeration, and that is not the way I want to be with them. Comments on the group process best come naturally from the member, if at all.

I feel much the same about process comments on the individual. To me, the *experience* of feeling competitive, for example, and experiencing that feeling openly, is more important than to have the facilitator put a label on this behaviour.

For some reason, I have no objection when a participant does something of this sort. For example, a faculty member was complaining about students who *always* want their questions answered, and *continuously* ask questions. He felt they just weren't adequately self-reliant. He kept insistently asking me, over and over, what to do about such behaviour. A group member finally said, 'You seem to be giving us a good example of just what you are complaining about.' This seemed very helpful.

I tend not to probe into or comment on what may be behind a person's behaviour. To me, an interpretation as to the *cause* of individual behaviour can never be anything but a high-level guess. The only way it can carry weight is when an authority puts his experience behind it. But I do not want to get involved in this kind of authoritativeness. 'I think it's because you feel inadequate as a man that you engage in this blustering behaviour,' is not the kind of statement I would ever make.

The Therapeutic Potentiality of the Group

If a very serious situation arises in a group, when an individual seems to be exhibiting psychotic behaviour or is acting in a bizarre way, I learned to rely on the members of the group to be as therapeutic or more therapeutic than I am myself. Sometimes as a professional one gets caught up in labels and feels, for example, 'This is straight paranoid behaviour!' As a consequence, one tends to withdraw somewhat and deal with the person more as an object. The more naïve group member, however, continues to relate to the troubled person as a *person*, and this is in my experience far more therapeutic. So, in situations in which a member is showing behaviour which is clearly pathological, I rely on the wisdom of the group more than on my own, and am often deeply astonished at the therapeutic ability of the members. This is both humbling and inspiring. It makes me realize what incredible potential for helping resides in the ordinary untrained person, if only he feels the freedom to use it.

Physical Movement and Contact

I express myself in physical movement as spontaneously as possible. My background is not such as to make me particularly free in this respect. But if I am restless I get up and stretch and move around; if I want to change places with another person, I ask him if he is willing. One may sit or lie on the floor if that meets one's physical needs. I do not particularly attempt, however, to promote physical movement in others, though there are facilitators who can do this beautifully and effectively.

Slowly I have learned to respond with physical contact when this seems real and spontaneous and appropriate. When a young woman was weeping because she had had a dream that no one in the group loved her, I embraced her and kissed and comforted her. When a person is suffering and I feel like going over and putting my arm around him, I do just that. Again, I do not try consciously to *promote* this kind of behaviour. I admire the younger people who are looser and freer in this respect.

A Three-Generational Viewpoint

After writing the above I had the opportunity to discuss non-verbal communication and physical contact with my daughter, Mrs Natalie R. Fuchs, and with one of my granddaughters, Anne B. Rogers, a college student. Natalie has often facilitated groups, and Anne had just returned from participating in an encounter group which she had found very valuable. They were both disappointed in the lack of stress I had given to these topics, and it occurred to me that an attempt to re-create the observations of each of them would give the perspective of three generations in one family on the issues of physical contact and other non-verbal means of communication. What follows is not verbatim, but a reasonably accurate account of each conversation, given in the first person, to make it clear they are speaking for themselves. Here first is Natalie Fuchs.

'I gained a great deal for myself, as a participant in groups, out of various physical and non-verbal experiences. Consequently, I have felt more free to initiate them in groups which I facilitate. I find that group members appreciate very much such new forms of communication, and they provide a great deal of data for consideration.

'I always participate myself in any of these experiences which I initiate. Personally, I find it hard to tell people what to do or even suggest what they might do, but I make it easier for myself by giving any member at any time the opportunity to opt out of such exercises. If I am a participant in a group, I want the freedom of choice – to risk myself in some suggested way or not. I don't like to get orders, so I don't give them.

'I think our culture has a terrible hang-up in this matter of touching. It only has one meaning and that is sexual – either heterosexual or homosexual. We deprive ourselves of much warmth and support by interpreting physical contact in this way. The group, however, provides a protected environment in which an individual can risk himself in these new ways and sort out his feelings about touch. A woman may find she wants a fatherly embrace from a man half her age, that she has homosexual feelings about another female, and is attracted sexually to a particular man. These feelings are all acceptable. Instead of being afraid of her emotions she can make rational choices based on her newly discovered feelings.

'It is important to me that non-verbal exercises meet the present needs or mood of the group or certain individuals in the group. If the members are in the initial stage of getting to know and trust one another, I suggest something that will help individuals reveal themselves at a fairly deep level.

'For example, people frequently start by introducing themselves in the cocktail party manner: "I'm a mother, a wife, a social worker." If this prevails I might suggest each person draw an abstract self-portrait or self-image with chalk. Pictures are tacked on the wall and explanations given. "This is the angry part of me – this red mess here – it's walled in most of the time but see, it breaks out here and there."

'Group members may ask questions about the picture but I put a stop to interpretations. The object of the exercise is to reveal *oneself*.

'Occasionally I use the following instructions to help a group get acquainted rapidly: "We seem to be having difficulty get-

T–C

ting beyond the socially accepted way of knowing each other. For those who wish to try something new I suggest we mill around introducing ourselves with a handshake, using our first names, and eye contact. (After a few minutes of this) Now stop using words and just shake hands and look at each other. (Later) Now stop shaking hands and find another way to say "hello".

'People gain much useful information about themselves and others which, if not used in the immediate follow-up discussion, is referred to in later sessions.

'I have found the blind walk – where one person leads around another who is blindfolded – a useful way of facing one's attitude towards dependence. There are many so-called "trust" exercises I have also used. The important thing to me is that these not be just party games but be used at the right time and the feelings explored.

'I have been co-leading a sensory awareness group for alienated teenagers. I use many procedures developed at Esalen. I am also a participant staff member with this same group in their weekly group therapy sessions. The "therapy hours" deal mostly with past experiences – relationships within the family, bad trips, attitudes towards school and society. The sensory awareness experience seems to supplement the therapy. It emphasizes the positive thing in life – the joy of smelling, touching, being aware, in the here and now, of another human being. It brings out the caring part of these young adults.

'One day a boy seemed quite out of it, very alone. I asked if there was anything we could do to bring him in. He replied, "Well, this has been an awfully rough week, at home and everywhere. What I'd really like is a body massage." So he lay on his belly and the other members crowded around him and massaged him thoroughly and lovingly. He seemed to experience the caring.

'Frequently something spontaneous happens non-verbally in a group if the norm has been established by the leader that such action is permissible.

'In an adult group one man was asking for feedback from the others. They were giving their impressions honestly in words. He seemed lonely, frightened and passive to me, both in his posture in the corner and what he had told us in previous sessions. When it was my turn to respond to him I asked him to move out of the corner and sit in front of me, where I could respond more directly. I couldn't resist giving him a slight push. He fell back and I pushed him lightly again and he fell back further. I began to feel angry and gave him a hard shove on the shoulder. We exchanged no words, but had been looking at each other. He finally fought back and we wrestled and struggled and I found I could not put him down. He gained a great deal from the experience and so did I. I believe, at least temporarily, he made more of a man of himself.

'We nearly always spend some time talking about the meanings we gain out of our non-verbal and physical contacts. It seems to me that there are several kinds of learnings which reappear. Perhaps one of the most important ones is that touch becomes "de-sexualized". It is not that it loses its sexual connotations, but these become less frightening, and touch acquires many new meanings. It also causes individuals to raise, at an experiential level, the question, "Do I truly wish to be *close* to another person?" Finally, since it is much easier to "con" others and even oneself with words, the non-verbal experiences raise the question, "Am I sincere? Do I mean what I say when I talk, or am I real only in my actions?" These are some of the values I have found in this sort of group experience.'

So much for Natalie's statement, from the viewpoint of a facilitator.

Here is the account by Anne, my granddaughter, of the body movement aspects of a week-end encounter group in which, for the first time, she felt enough trust in a group to express herself freely in physical ways. This account, like the rest, is a reconstruction of some of our conversation.

'John, one of the members, had had experience in psychodrama and body movement in previous groups. At first he antagonized all of us by seeming to think he was superior, but somehow at the end of our first evening session — perhaps he started it — we all moved into the centre of the room, a tight mass of bodies, with our arms around each other, and swayed back and forth with our eyes closed. It was a remarkable feeling, and by the next day we all felt more free to be in physical contact when we wanted to be.

'It would be hard to tell all of the ways in which we used physical means to express our feelings. At times we sat very close together on the floor, sometimes holding hands. Sometimes members who were angry at each other pushed against each other – hard. Once there was an angry wrestling match in which we hovered around to protect, if necessary, either of the two men, or the room. But there were very tender movements too – people hugging and embracing each other. We also went on a "trust walk". At one point we expressed our feelings to the woman facilitator by gently swaying her back and forth. One evening we got to feeling silly and expressed that too – by dancing around like apes! It was fun to just let things out, as they came.

'There were two men in our group who were really afraid of touching. One was a married man who felt he was in some way not being fair to his wife if he touched or showed tender feelings towards the women in the group. He gradually changed in this respect. The other was a tense young guy who seemed to believe that if he didn't control his feelings very tightly – especially his angry and sexual feelings – he would fly completely out of control.

'With this second man, when he was speaking very emotionally about a problem in his family somewhat similar to a problem in mine, I began to cry. I just went over and cried on his shoulder. Afterwards it seemed to me that this had helped him realize that physical contact with a girl didn't necessarily mean sex. Later we were able to discuss some of the ways his intensity frightens girls.

'I think something of what all this meant to me is contained in some notes I made shortly after the group. They are very rough, but you can use them if you want.' (I have chosen some of her notes, since space does not permit quoting them all.)

Verbal communication; so necessary; but words are also a barrier; can be used particularly to fend off contact. And if I want to express things, myself, in another way, what can I do? Can I reach you, reach out to you? With eyes, touch, smile?

We all walk around trying not to bump into people; so much energy expended in avoidance.

But there is nothing so beautiful and beautifully human as to be held, hugged, loved. To feel the warmth and sincerity of another person. To give, in turn, comfort, strength. Words can often deceive; but an embrace — the truth is conveyed by something other than sound . . .

Why are we so afraid to touch? Because to touch means — SEX.

But don't you see? There is no black or white; but a whole continuum in between. Yes, touching, holding, hugging, carries sex. The most distant, coldly executed handshake is sexual, even in its denial of emotion. The way to deal with touching is not to de-sex it, but acknowledge the existence of sensuousness; accept it. If I can accept the experience of contact, I will no longer be troubled by it. If I accept the responses it touches off in me, I will probably discover not fear, repulsion; but the true content of the hug — love, warmth, joy.

When I'm in a situation where I'm uncertain about movement; in a group or even with an individual; when I want to reach out to someone and hold his or her hand just to let them know I understand — but there is doubt of the reception; then I feel tight and knotted up inside; as if I were sitting on some volcano, holding down an eruption. What a miserable feeling! My mind is in control, saying, 'Don't be foolish; why reach out, you'll be rejected; the other person will be uncomfortable, making you feel awkward; everyone will be wondering about your intentions; don't be so conspicuous.' So I sit there and feel tight, and anxious, and fearful; and wishing I could be free.

It's so natural, lovely, to be warm and genuine. Spontaneously to feel life, acknowledge and *share* it.

This has been a rather lengthy digression, but I hope it has been helpful in pointing out, not only a trend in encounter groups, but a trend in our culture. It is very clear that Natalie, my daughter, is much freer than I in using movement and contact in groups she facilitates. It is certainly clear to me that as a college student I could not possibly have held the sentiments nor written the notes produced by Anne, my granddaughter. So both encounter groups, and the times, are changing.

Now that I have presented this three-level view of the way in which physical means may be encouraged by a facilitator and experienced by a participant, I would like to turn to certain other issues involved in my way of being in a group.

Some Faults of Which I Am Aware

I am much better in a group in which feelings are being expressed – any kind of feelings – than in an apathetic group. I am not particularly good in provoking a relationship, and have real admiration for some facilitators I know who can readily provoke a real and meaningful relationship, which then continues to develop. I frequently choose such a person as a co-facilitator.

As I noted briefly above, I am often slow to sense and express my own anger. Consequently, I may only become aware of it and express it later. In a recent encounter group I was at different times very angry with two individuals. With one I was not conscious of it until the middle of the night and had to wait until the next morning to express it. With the other, I was able to realize and express it in the session in which it occurred. In both instances it led to real communication – to a strengthening of the relationship and gradually to the feeling of genuine liking for each other. But I am a slow learner in this area and consequently have a real appreciation of what others go through as they try to relax their defences sufficiently to let immediate feelings of the moment seep through into awareness.

A Special Problem

In recent years I have had to deal with a problem which is special to anyone who has become rather widely known through writings and through being taught about in classrooms. People come into a group with me with all kinds of expectations – from a halo over my head to sprouting horns. I try to dissociate myself as rapidly as possible from these hopes or fears. In dress, manner, and by expressing my wish that they get to know me as a person – not simply as a name or a book or a theory – I try to *become* a person to the members of the group. It is always refreshing to find myself in a gathering – for

example, of high school girls, or sometimes of businessmen —
for whom I am not a 'name' and where I have to 'make it' all
over again simply as the person I am. I could have kissed the
young girl who said challengingly at the start of a group, 'I
think this sounds like kind of a risky thing. What are your
qualifications for doing this?' I replied that I had had some
experience in working with groups and hoped they would find
me qualified, but that I could certainly understand her concern,
and they would have to form their own judgement of me.

Behaviour Which I Believe To Be Non-Facilitative[3]

Though I stressed at the outset of this chapter that there are
many effective styles of working with a group, there are also a
number of people who conduct groups whom I do not recommend, because some of their approach seems to me non-
facilitative, or even damaging, to a group and its members. I
cannot conclude this discussion in an honest way without list-
ing some of these behaviours. Research is in such an infant
stage in this field that one cannot pretend that opinions such as
those expressed below are factually based or supported by research findings. These are simply opinions which have grown
out of my experience, and are expressed as such.

1. I am definitely suspicious of the person who appears to be
exploiting the present interest in groups. Because of the enormously expanding interest, a number of workers seem to me to
have as their slogans, 'Get publicity fast!' 'Get on the band-
wagon!' When such traits appear in individuals who are working with people, I am deeply offended.

2. A facilitator is less effective when he pushes a group,
manipulates it, makes rules for it, tries to direct it towards his
own unspoken goals. Even a slight flavour of this kind can
either diminish (or destroy) the group's trust in him, or — even
worse — make the members his worshipful followers. If he has
specific goals, he had best make them explicit.

3. Then there is the facilitator who judges the success or
failure of a group by its dramatics — who counts the number of

3. In writing this section I have profited by discussion with many individuals, but particularly Ann Dreyfuss and William R. Coulson.

people who have wept or those who have been 'turned on'. For me, this leads towards a highly spurious evaluation.

4. I do not recommend a facilitator who believes in some one single line of approach as the *only* essential element in the group process. For one, 'attacking defences' is the sine qua non. For another, 'drawing out the basic rage in every person' is his one-note song. I have a great deal of respect for Synanon and the effectiveness of their work with drug addicts, but am repelled by their hastily formed dogma that unrelenting attack, whether based on real or spurious feelings, is the criterion by which a group is to be judged successful or unsuccessful. I want hostility or rage to be expressed when it is present, and want to express them myself when they are genuinely present in me, but there are *many* other feelings, and they have equal significance in living and in the group.

5. I cannot recommend as facilitator a person whose own problems are so great and pressing that he needs to centre the group on himself and is not available to, nor deeply aware of, others. Such a person might well be a participant in a group, but it is unfortunate when he carries the label of 'facilitator'.

6. I do not welcome as facilitator a person who frequently gives interpretations of motives or causes of behaviour in members of the group. If these are inaccurate they are of no help; if deeply accurate, they may arouse extreme defensiveness, or even worse, strip the person of his defences, leaving him vulnerable and possibly hurt as a person, particularly after the group sessions are over. Such statements as 'You certainly have a lot of latent hostility,' or 'I think you're compensating for your essential lack of masculinity' can fester in an individual for months, causing great lack of confidence in his own ability to understand himself.

7. I do not like it when a facilitator introduces exercises or activities with some such statement as, 'Now we will all —'. This is simply a special form of manipulation, but very difficult for the individual to resist. If exercises are introduced, I think any member should have the opportunity, clearly stated by the facilitator, to opt out of the activity.

8. I do not like the facilitator who withholds himself from personal emotional participation in the group — holding himself

aloof as the expert, able to analyse the group process and members' reactions through superior knowledge. This is often seen in individuals who make their living by conducting groups, but seems to show both a defensiveness in themselves and a deep lack of respect for the participants. Such a person denies his own spontaneous feelings and provides a model for the group – that of the overly cool analytical person who never gets involved – which is the complete antithesis of what I believe in. That is what each participant will then naturally aim to achieve: the exact opposite of what I should hope for. Non-defensiveness and spontaneity – not the defence of aloofness – are what I personally hope will emerge in a group.

Let me make clear that I do not object at all to the qualities I have mentioned in any *participant* in the group. The individual who is manipulative, or over-interpretative, or totally attacking, or emotionally aloof, will be very adequately handled by the group members themselves. They will simply not permit such behaviours to continue persistently. But when the facilitator exhibits these behaviours, he tends to set a norm for the group before the members have learned that they can confront and deal with him as well as with each other.

CONCLUSION

I have tried here to describe the manner in which I would like to behave as the perceived facilitator of a group. I do not always succeed in carrying out my own personal aims, and then the experience tends to be less satisfying to the group members and to myself. I have also described some of the behaviour which I regard as non-facilitative. I sincerely hope that this presentation will encourage others to speak for their own styles of group facilitation.

4

Change after Encounter Groups: in Persons, in Relationships, in Organizations

There is a great deal of debate as to whether the intensive group experience produces any significant change, and especially whether it produces any *lasting* change, in behaviour. In this chapter I should like to consider its influence on individual behaviour, on individuals in their relationships, and on the policies and structures of the organizations to which many of them belong. These issues will be explored primarily on the basis of my own experience, reserving to a later section discussion of the limited knowledge so far gained from research.

For some reason I find myself wanting to state the conclusions first – a very poor mode of presentation! Later I hope to convey some feeling for the personal and phenomenological data on which these tentative conclusions rest.

I should perhaps stress that I am basing my statements largely on experience with groups facilitated by my colleagues and myself. Our emphasis is, I believe, slightly different from that which is popular today. As is evident from the foregoing chapter, we are most receptive and understanding rather than manipulative; we tend to place our trust in the group and group process rather than in the charismatic power of the leader; we hope there will be both verbal and non-verbal communication, but do not side with one or the other; we wish the group members to develop their own individualized goals rather than having some pre-set goal such as happiness, joy, or effective organizational behaviour; we expect the group process to be painful if it leads towards growth – in fact, believe all growth is turbulent and disturbing as well as satisfying. We do not believe the group experience, no matter how uplifting, to be an end in itself, but find its significance primarily in the influence it has on later behaviour outside the group. Thus we represent only a part of the vast spectrum of special theories, practices, devices, exercises, and emphases which characterize the group movement today. So, asking the question from my perspective, as I have tried to describe it: What changes have *I* seen in *individuals*, following experience in an encounter group?

Individual Change

Many images and memories flood in on me as I try to answer this query. Here are the thoughts that emerge. I have seen individuals alter, very measurably, their concepts of themselves, as they explore their feelings in an accepting climate, and receive tough and tender feedback from group members who care. I have seen persons begin to realize and bring into being more of their own potential, through their behaviours both in the group and afterwards. Time and time again, I have seen individuals choose a whole new direction for their lives – philosophically, vocationally, and intellectually – as a result of an encounter group experience. Some persons go through an encounter group *untouched*, experiencing *no* significant change, then or later. Some persons *seemingly* uninvolved in such a group show change later, in most interesting behavioural ways. Two individuals, out of the many hundreds in groups I have conducted, have shown what I regard as negative change – one undergoing a temporary psychotic break after the group, the other (who had displayed, I later learned, many psychotic symptoms before the group) undergoing a full-fledged psychosis. Both experiences occurred more than twenty years ago and would, I think, be less likely to happen in a group of mine today. A number of individuals have sought individual or group psychotherapy following an encounter group. In some instances this seemed a most positive step, leading to growth, while in others it is a reasonable question whether the experience brought such rapid and painful change that the individual was *forced* to seek further help. This last I personally regard as unfortunate.

Let me turn to my second question and again give a highly summarized answer. What changes have I seen in the *relationships* of persons in and/or following an encounter group? I have known individuals for whom the encounter experience has meant an almost miraculous change in the depth of their communication with spouse and children. Sometimes for the first time real feelings are shared. This has happened most dramatically where participants have returned home each night, or where they have been members of a couples or family group. Thus they are able to share their growing insights, take the risk of expressing their real feelings, both loving and negative, as soon as they themselves have become aware of them. A great deal of sleep is lost in this process, but the growth in relationship is extraordinary. I have seen fathers who went home, able for the first time in years to communicate with their sons, mothers with their children. I have seen teachers who have transformed their classrooms, following an encounter experience, into a personal, caring, trusting, learning group, where students participate fully and openly in forming the curriculum and all the other aspects of their education. Tough business executives, who described a particular business relationship as hopeless, have gone home and changed it into a constructive one. Students in a seminary where love and brotherhood were the verbal ideals – contrasting sharply with the reality of complete and lonely alienation – have made tremendous strides towards real communication and caring for one another.

There have been situations where one spouse, gaining greatly in insight and openness, has gone home after an encounter group and so frightened and threatened the other with his or her spontaneity that the communication gap has become temporarily – in some cases permanently – increased. Sometimes couples face, in a group, the buried differences between them, and frequently reach a real reconciliation; at other times they realize openly that there is a gap they cannot bridge. It is fair to say that I have often seen tremendous changes in the relationships of persons – mostly constructive, but sometimes negative from a social, though not necessarily a personal, point of view.

Organizational Change

And what changes have there been in organizational policies and structure, following encounter groups? Here my experience leads to more moderate and cautious statements. I have seen situations in which *individuals* were greatly changed, and their *institutions* changed scarcely at all. Teachers may go through deeply moving growth experiences, but in their next faculty meeting show little if any shift from the sterile meetings of the past. On the other hand, I have seen faculties drop grading systems, place students on all committees, and open up channels of administrator-faculty-student communication as a result of encounter group experiences. Policies of budget formation in a college have been completely altered. Presidents and provosts and deans have modified their administrative procedures in more human directions.

Business executives will sometimes change such stressful and judgemental practices as 'periodic evaluation of subordinates' into a humanly *mutual* and constructive feedback. I have seen interpersonal communication become the heart and core of a business enterprise – and have also come to recognize that encounter groups, because they foster individual independence, openness and integrity, are *not* conducive to unquestioning institutional loyalty. Business executives have resigned their jobs; priests and nuns, ministers and professors, have left their orders and churches and universities because of the courage gained in such groups, deciding to work for change outside the institution rather than within it. There have been changes in an educational institution, fostered by encounter groups, splitting the faculty into antagonistic parties of those who wanted change and those who resisted it. In short, while change and growth *often* introduce turbulence into the life of the individual, they seem almost *inevitably* to induce it in institutions – a most threatening experience to the traditional administrator.

The Basis for These Tentative Conclusions

I seem to be making this presentation backwards, but somehow it comes naturally in this order. The above are lessons learned and tentative findings formulated from my experience.

What is that experience? I have tried to engage in a broad spectrum of encounter groups, with closely related consultant activity, in order to increase my own learning. I have had a three-year continuous consulting experience with the administration, faculty, and students of Cal Tech, from which I learned a great deal. Another major experience was a three-year association with the schools conducted or supervised by the Order of the Immaculate Heart – college, high schools, and elementary schools. I have had all-too-brief experiences – from two to five days – with the administrators and some faculty members of the six Claremont Colleges; with a number of trustees, administrators, faculty, and students of Columbia University; with the faculty and students of thirteen junior colleges; with the counselling staff of several colleges; with presidents of large corporations; with business executives at various levels; with nurses – administrative, teaching, and supervisory; with religious workers of many denominations; with ghetto black and brown 'consumers' of health services and health agency 'providers' of medical services (a most exciting confrontation and dialogue); with mental health workers in all categories; and finally, with university classes taught in encounter group fashion. The types of group involved have been so-called encounter groups, personal development groups, task-oriented groups, consultant groups. I have led 'stranger' groups and gatherings of working colleagues; also adolescent and couples groups. These have taken place in Australia, Japan, and France as well as in the United States. Lacking in my experience have been groups composed of families, of elementary school children, of elderly adults. But, all in all, I have been very fortunate in meeting with an exceedingly wide range of individuals, in many different settings. I have tried to be as observant and open as possible, and the formulations given above are the best I have been able to make of this wide experience.

An Instance of Individual Change

As I continue to more or less back into this presentation – giving last the data which should presumably come first – another quandary arises. I have jotted down many instances of deep personal change observed. One is tempted to multiply these examples. But the effect might well be unconvincing, a sort of a salesman's talk, overwhelming the reader with brief, indigestible items. I have chosen instead to give *one* example in which, almost five years after the event, a man describes the attitudes with which he approached the encounter group, his experiences in it, and the subsequent changes in his behaviour, life goals, and personality. Here is the letter from a man I shall call Joe:

DEAR CARL,

I am going to try and express as clearly and accurately as possible the changes that have occurred in my life as a result of my first encounter group experience, nearly five years ago. The changes have been many and cumulative, and have seemed to run in a consistent direction, one getting me ready for, and leading me to the next.

As I go back in memory and recapture the experience of the week-long workshop with you, I begin to get excited all over again, and actually feel the emotions I had then. I was thrilled to be enrolled in the workshop, but I had no idea what I was really getting into. I did not know what an encounter group was. I had never heard of one. I only knew that I really valued your psychology and your philosophy. It fitted so well with my own sensibilities. And I was thrilled to think that I would be sitting at the feet of the 'master' for a whole week. Undoubtedly some of the charisma would 'rub off'.

We began on Monday. By Wednesday I was really confused. I couldn't for the life of me figure out what was going on. And I was silent. After I got over the initial shock of a direct critical remark made by one of the participants about a man sitting next to me, I sat in wonder, and in fear, and in growing excitement at the interaction that was taking place all around me. It was as if something new, and intriguing, and intoxicating, as well as frightening, was becoming real all around me. I began asking myself if this were all real, or if we were just playing fun and games. I believe that that was the first real comment I made. 'Are we for real? Or are we just playing fun and games?' I remember saying (this was about Wednesday) that I wasn't sure that I wanted to know the members of the group at all, and I really wasn't sure I wanted them to know me.

Once I had said that I was 'in' the group and the most marvelous thing began to happen. The last two days seemed like a beautiful birth to a new existence. It was as if so many of the things that I valued in word were becoming true for me in fact. It is extremely difficult to describe the experience. I had not known how unaware I was of my deepest feelings nor how valuable they might be to other people. Only when I began to express what was rising from some-where deep within the centre of me, and saw the tears in the eyes of the other group members because *I* was saying something so true for them too, did I begin to really feel that I was deeply a part of the human race. Never in my life before that group experience had I experienced 'me' so intensely. And then to have that 'me' so confirmed and loved by the group, who by this time were sensitive and reacting to my phoniness, was like receiving a gift I could never have hoped for, because until then I never dreamed that it could exist.

I discovered that when I expressed me, the deeper *feeling* me, whom I had always hid, I contributed something unique, beautiful and lifegiving to several others in the group. I couldn't believe it. But I couldn't deny it either, because the evidence was so clear and strong. I remember feeling very strongly that I had discovered the world of persons for the first time, and that when I could really be *me*, and get past the things that made me fear or dislike other persons, I could only love them and be loved by them.

Although I have since passed through some very painful periods of growth in my life I can never deny the reality of the positive hope I carry with me because of the profound experience of humanness that I shared in the first group: humanness that is both personally mine and that I share with other persons, no matter how closed up they may be.

And so how has my life changed because of that first encounter group experience? Vocationally it has not changed at all. I was in the seminary at that time and have since been ordained a priest. But within my vocation as a priest there have been profound changes both inside me and outside me. Inside, I began to grow from a boy to a man. Outside I became much freer in relation to authority and human respect. Inside me I was so much more present to myself and therefore to others that my work as a counselor and a therapist shot up one hundred per cent in its effectiveness. I had been trying so hard to be an effective counselor; being congruent, showing empathy and positive regard, really listening to the other person. And while I was somewhat effective, there seemed to be low limits to what would happen in counseling sessions.

During the time of the workshop I was involved in a counseling practicum, and the difference between what happened in the counseling office after I had experienced the encounter group and what had happened before was totally amazing to me. All of a sudden everything that I had learned in theory was happening, and without my expending a great deal of energy to make it happen. I was present. I heard. I was able to risk me and some of my own feelings, and the client suddenly opened up and got in touch with himself or herself in a whole new way. All of a sudden the counseling process was operating, as it had never operated for me before. I guess I should say that *I* was operating in a way in which I had never functioned before. And it all seemed so natural and real. There was no artificiality.

I have not maintained the same high degree of functioning at all times since. Sometimes I am better, sometimes I am worse, but after the workshop I have never been the same person I was as I walked into the group that first day. Since the group I have continued to train as a counselor and therapist. And I have had many more encounter group experiences and now function as a group facilitator.

Instead of becoming a high school principal, as was scheduled for me, I was switched into the field of counseling psychology and I am now getting a doctor's degree in Human Behavior. It became obvious to me and to others in positions of authority that I should stay in the field of persons and interpersonal relationships rather than go into administration. At the time the decision was made to switch I would have made a very bad administrator, but had the potentialities to become a very good counselor and therapist. Now, while I am trying to continue the process started in that first group experience, I have discovered some of the personality inadequacies that would have made me a bad administrator and have begun to work on those.

I suppose if I were to zero in on the most significant change that has occurred in my life because of the encounter experience I would have to say that I really began to take more definite shape as a person. I began to have and own a clearer definition of myself. Some of what emerged was not pleasant to recognize, but it was part of a whole that was acceptable to others and more and more so to me. I began to own my own person: that person who so often felt like a little boy in a world of grown-up men, who felt fear and let that fear inhibit him from really being fully alive and functional in relationships with other persons. And as I began really to be responsible for that 'little boy' part of me, he began to grow up and get strong or maybe he began to lose his hold on me. Anyway I began to become. It's about the only way I can say it. I had to give up some of the comforts of being a small and helpless boy and take on more and more of the responsibilities of being a growing man, but what a joy that has been.

Since that first encounter I have learned some very experiential lessons. I have a greater faith in persons. I know that other people are like me deep down inside. I know that I share a very real beautiful, sometimes painful existence with them. I have so much more hope in the future of man. Because if we can touch one another as persons the way it can happen in an encounter, then 'redemption' begins to happen for all of us, and we emerge from a death-like existence of loneliness and diminution to a possibility of fully-aliveness. I can really say 'yes' to mankind, because I have discovered in a deeply personal way, in a way that I can deeply feel as well as think, that each person in the world is an abundant reservoir of life and love that only needs to be tapped to be made available for self-nourishment and for the refreshment of others. I know it too often does not happen because of our defensiveness and fear, but I know it *can* happen, *has* happened and *will* happen. And that makes all the difference.

Sincerely and affectionately,
JOE

This man's experience has been mostly positive, though he does mention some of the very painful periods of growth during these five years. For some, change has been even more painful, as will be evident in the chapter, 'The Person in Change'.

The testimony of people like these gives me a gut-level conviction that profound personal and behavioural change can and does occur in and following an encounter group experience. Clearly, changes of this depth do not occur in every person. Moreover, what little research has been done is somewhat contradictory on this point, though significant change in the self-concept does seem fairly well established. But if two or three or five people show dramatic and lasting change after an encounter group — change in the direction of becoming more aware persons, more fully functioning persons — then I shall continue to be impressed by the fact, even though changes in the other members may not be so profound.

Examples of Change in Relationships

Three examples follow of the way in which people can relate differently after an encounter group. The first illustrates beautifully how children will sense a change in feeling and attitude, even when outer behaviour seems scarcely to have changed at all. A mother who had been in a group with a colleague of mine wrote him shortly after the group was over:

> As you know, things are pretty peachy-keen with Pete, my husband, and me. But, as you probably noticed, I never did say that about the children. I was bothered about the squabbling between Marie and Alice. I was bothered about Marie's bed-wetting. I was bothered that I couldn't give them a lot of affection. I was bothered because they never really talked to me. I was bothered by some of the hurtful things Pete and I could say to them. So, when I came floating home Sunday with this new real self, I was anticipating a response of sorts. What I didn't anticipate was the quickness and the intensity of the response.

Shortly after she got home, it was bedtime for Marie, the ten-year-old younger daughter. Her mother asked Marie if she could scrub her.

> In the space of an hour we talked about menstruation, God, the Devil, Heaven, Hell, hating someone so much you wanted them dead, stealing candy from the kitchen, nightmares, monsters in the window. Of course we had talked about these things before, but never with such completeness. Alice, who is fifteen months older than Marie, came wandering into the bathroom and shared this experience with us. I ended up scrubbing her also. This surprised me – that she wanted me to bathe her – as her body is becoming adolescent and she is very self-conscious about this. Marie said, 'What did you do at that meeting – learn how to be nice to kids?' I said, 'No, I learned how to be myself, which is really pretty nice.'

A second example is a letter written to Bill and Audrey McGaw, a year after they had conducted a group for engaged and married couples. It speaks for itself. The man begins:

> This is a letter that I have started to write one hundred times. It is about what happened and what is happening. It is filled with love. It is filled with tears and joy and love.

As I sit here now writing to you tears well up in my eyes and I am overcome by emotion. I have never before been able to write a letter like this. This is what I want to say. This is to thank you, to let you know that you passed it on, you did your job. The time was right, and I picked it up and now I have it and I'll never lose it, and I'm passing it on.

Eileen and I are married, and Eileen and I are living together, and we have problems, and we fight and we bitch and we love one another. We would not have this today if we hadn't met you both. But we did meet you, we spent several days together and we broke through. It's not perfect, but it happened at the right time, and we were fortunate to meet with the right people, we were ready and you changed the path of our lives. We now know what is possible and achievable. This base, this emotional security in our marriage has provided for me a springboard, an opening, a vantage point. Open, flowing, pouring ... words cannot adequately describe what has really happened to me. You know what it is. I have it! It's wild!

I know now why I've waited so long to write. Now I'm certain. It has been over one year and now the fear is gone. I will never lose what I now have. I realize that what I have merely puts me in a position of accepting greater responsibilities. Now I understand why you, Audrey, and you, Bill, must go through what you go through with each group.

I should like to add one more picture – that of a teacher and her pupils. An elementary school teacher who had been in an encounter group some months before was asked by letter what, if any, outcome there had been for her. She writes,

You asked what happened to me ... pure and simple, someone got to me – the *inside* me. I listened and I heard, have heard and have been hearing things I have never listened to before ... and love it. Results? All I know is it's fun. I have *listened* to my students. I asked them if in the past I had turned any off or not listened. The biggest *thugs* in the class all raised their hands. Also – they are the most sensitive ... I have had the busiest, most arousing, sapping, exciting, fun-filled, fulfilling, and happiest months since I started teaching and it hasn't stopped yet.

Her observation about the problem students, the 'thugs' as she calls them, is particularly interesting. It is often true that youngsters who are creating problems are more sensitive to interpersonal relationships than others. Her comment also raises the interesting question of cause and effect. Were these children 'thugs', and did she consequently feel they were not worth listening to, or did they *become* 'thugs' because they felt they were not heard? It opens up a whole new perspective of thought on so-called problem youngsters in the classroom. Her statement also suggests how involved both students and teachers can become in learning when communication is *real* between teachers and students.

I don't wish to be misunderstood on these examples. Such things do not happen to every mother, or every couple, or every teacher. But that they happen frequently makes the encounter a most exciting and potent interpersonal experience. It can help to free people to be spontaneous, and angry, and loving, and sensitively aware of life. In short, it can permit persons to become truly human in their relationships with one another.

An Example of Organizational Change

There are also a dozen instances of significant change in the attitudes, policies, and structures of institutions, from which I have chosen only one. It leads to a very mixed conclusion. I wish I could relate it with the vividness with which it was reported to me.[1]

A certain boy's high school managed by a Catholic order had been a prestige school of high academic standards and morale, in a middle- or upper-middle-class white suburb. Over a decade the neighbourhood had changed drastically; at the time of this report the school was 75 per cent Mexican-American, 20 per cent black, and 5 per cent Oriental and Caucasian. It had become a ghetto school in a ghetto neighbourhood. Standards had fallen, morale was low, apathy and alienation had crept in, the 'drug scene' was an important part of the ethos, and involvement by students was almost nil. In spite of this there were, so far as the faculty was concerned, no serious problems with the school, for the tight discipline enforced by the Order

1. I am greatly indebted to a long-time teacher in this school for a complete report on the events which I summarize here.

kept a semblance of conventional education as a comfortable façade.

All this broke wide open during and following a school dance, at which students – particularly the student leaders – blatantly brought, used, and distributed alcohol and drugs. As if this were not enough, the student body as a whole united in trying to conceal all these activities from the faculty. The rift between students and school was complete.

The beginning of change was inaugurated by the principal when he suspended classes, called a meeting of the whole school, and said in effect, 'We all know we have a serious problem. Let's talk about it.' His own openness and that of other faculty encouraged dialogue and discussion. First it was criticism by 'good' students of 'bad' students for behaviour at the dance. But gradually the students took the risk of discussing deeper issues: their lives were futile and drugs were appealing; classes were boring; studies were irrelevant to their lives; teachers were uninterested; discipline was repressive; dress codes made no sense in the students' world; there was no emphasis on the history and identity of minority groups. These topics were passionately discussed, and not squelched. Dedicated faculty members remained open and non-defensive, though clearly jolted and hurt. The meeting ended on a note of hope.

The upshot was that, during the brief remainder of the school year and during the summer, faculty and students worked together on the problems. Then, in some desperation, four members of the counselling staff, which had been under particular fire, enrolled in the summer training programme for group facilitators made available by the Center for Studies of the Person in La Jolla. Their experience in the encounter groups in that programme was so enriching that they felt greatly strengthened in their desire to remain open in communication, to trust the students, to encourage them to participate in all educational and administrative aspects of the school, and to introduce an encounter group atmosphere into all aspects of high school communication, policy-making, and even classrooms.

The results of these efforts, both before and after the encounter group experience of these four faculty members, were startling. The faculty stated that they would trust the students to be *responsible for themselves* in matters of attendance, tardiness, conduct, drugs, dress, and grooming. Students were expected to become involved in the school in a manner acceptable to their peers. If their conduct was not acceptable, the students were responsible. Seventy elected students and all the faculty (even the maintenance staff) had their expenses paid to meet for three full days at a rustic resort out of town, where plans were made for the coming year. This made it evident that the faculty was not kidding. They *meant* what they said.

The opening of this school in the fall was in stark contrast to that of neighbouring ghetto schools. In the public schools, police and private security guards were much in evidence, as were fear and hostility. In parochial schools, the opening sessions were devoted to setting forth the strict rules, the penalties for breaking them, and the organizational procedures. At this school, however, students were told that they were trusted, that they would certainly make mistakes, and that the important thing was to learn from mistakes.

What was the outcome?

First, some of the more controversial aspects. Some other schools refused to play with teams from this one, because some of its athletes had long hair, sideburns, and moustaches! (The students had felt that all these were natural in their culture.) Strong ethnic activist groups (Black Student Union and United Mexican-American Students) were formed. They wore berets and emblems. They demonstrated. They brought intense criticism from a shocked community – a fear and criticism which continued. But as these groups found that their creative thinking and influence and power was welcomed in the school, their more extreme behaviour diminished.

As the year wore on, many faculty members simply could not take the new policy, until by the end of the year the faculty was profoundly divided. A great many left, and there was a deep flavour of bitterness in what had been a united school. This was so marked that some of those who had helped to inaugurate the new policy felt it had been a failure and were thoroughly discouraged.

Such doubts did not have much effect upon the students. Attendance, since it was not required, increased greatly. Tardiness simply disappeared as a serious problem. The drug problem – certainly on the school grounds – sharply decreased. Classes which had been dull and boring were enlivened through pungent discussion by disadvantaged youth, and faculty members had to struggle to keep up. Most incredible of all, many seniors applied to, and gained, scholarships to four-year colleges – this in a ghetto school from which almost *no one* ever went to college.

I do not want to understate the problems. Some faculty endeavoured to return to the authoritarian methods of the past, with very divisive results. It became clear that freedom can rarely be revoked. Some teachers were afraid of the new and unknown path on which they had embarked. The very small minority of white students became, in many cases, hardened and hostile towards what was going on. The parents were disturbed and upset by the new developments, and it was difficult to communicate to them the new philosophy and its rationale. There can be no doubt that the school was more disorganized, more chaotic, during this year than it had been before.

To me this illustrates in very brief form many of the things I have learned about self-directed institutional change. Encounter group experiences, and an encounter group type of atmosphere in an institution, can definitely bring about highly constructive change, but may also create sharp division between members of the establishment; may be upsetting to the community; may be deeply threatening to those who are bound by tradition, and may thus raise the question whether constructive change or disaster has occurred. Yet the group about which we should be *most* concerned, those who are being *served* by the school, have in overwhelming majority found it to be a freeing, releasing, life-giving, involving, responsible learning experience. So while change might have occurred more slowly and with less pain, and mistakes were made that might have been avoided (for example, by more emphasis on group follow-up), the result appears to be positive. Open and honest communication, of feelings as well as thoughts; recognition of students, faculty, and administration as having a basic equality as persons; encountering each other on the real issues of the organization, does bring real and probably irreversible change.

A drastic and controversial instance of organizational change was chosen here, partly to show the potency of the spirit of trust engendered in the encounter group. One might select much more moderate illustrations.

I hope I have presented enough raw data to indicate that the beliefs stated at the outset are not illusory. Experience in an encounter group can set in motion profound changes within the individual person and his behaviour; in a variety of human relationships; and in the policies and structure of an organization.

5

The Person in Change:
The Process as Experienced

Here is a sample of the sort of comment a facilitator receives a week or two following an encounter group experience. 'The insights are still coming ... I haven't noticed a tremendous change in myself ... but I do seem to have opened some kind of a door that was closed before.' Such a statement seems positive, but what does it actually signify, now and later, in the life of the individual who makes it? We have seen in the last chapter some of the changes that may occur. Not much attention was paid, however, to the *process* by which later change comes about.

I want here to make use of a rare and fortuitous circumstance – a series of letters extending over a period of more than six years – to try to illuminate, almost microscopically, the fluctuating stages by which individual change develops.

The Group – and Ellen

Some years ago I was a facilitator for a group of business executives on the East Coast, composed of thirteen men and two women. We met at an inn in a very comfortable resort setting for five and a half days. Many meaningful things went on during those days for each person involved, including myself, but I cannot possibly describe all these events. I shall turn instead to those that happened later in the life of one member, an unmarried woman executive.

Ellen (the name is fictitious, as are all names in this account) was the head of a small technical business. She was rather quiet in the group, though she did get into some sharp disagreements with two of the men. She talked at some length about the problems she was having with one of the executives in her business, Liz, a woman with whom she had quite a complex working relationship, involving Ellen as executive and Liz as subordinate, and also a personal dependency of Ellen on Liz, who was a strong and somewhat dominating woman. Towards the very end of the week she also made some mention of the difficulties involved in living with her mother. But if my memory is accurate she explored this problem very little, and I at least was not sensitive enough to realize that it was a major problem in her life. I thought the group was of some assistance to her in the question of dealing with Liz, her employee, but do not think that any great help was given in regard to her relationship with her mother. On the next-to-last day of the group, Ellen received some fairly strenuous feedback, both disturbing and enlightening to her, which made her highly emotional and tearful. The way in which group members help each other is well illustrated by a caring note given to her afterwards by one member, a complete stranger to her when the week began. I did not know of it until much later, when she wrote me how she had treasured it. This is best quoted here as a part of her group experience.

As your friend, I applaud and affirm all that you are, the very idea and core of your existence, your being you and the specialness of your unique individuality. My task as your friend is to help you be the most that you can be of you, to extend to you the freedom and encouragement of my relatedness to you and of yours to me. I care for you, but I will never own you nor use you, for you are your own person, never to be owned by anyone else – though you may belong and others may belong to you as I do. I am all for you in all ways and am always with you, though we might be continents apart. Never will I leave you, nor do you ever have in any way to earn my love. You have that because you are you – and because I find this such a wonderful something to be.

Small wonder that Ellen found this man's note very precious.

Though she did not say a great deal at the time regarding her mother, I must have partially sensed the depth of that problem, for I remember that in bidding her farewell I said, 'I hope that on the Fourth of July (about a month away) you will be celebrating *your* declaration of independence.'

Since there is often a great deal of question raised as to what happens to people after encounter groups, it is satisfying to be able to indicate what happend to this one person, since it can be documented through her letters. Certainly hers is not the average experience, but neither, according to my knowledge, is it strikingly unusual.

Less than two weeks following the end of the group, Ellen wrote me that she had had a wonderful note from her room-mate at the inn. This woman had been in another group, and Ellen had helped her through some difficult periods during that week. She reported her room-mate as saying, '. . . the days since we all parted have been full of ideas and feelings I haven't had before in my life, and I think many of the seemingly disjointed discoveries about myself over the last years have finally begun to fall into place. I'm about bursting with differences from the old me, and I credit the experience at the Inn with lighting the fuse that has long been smouldering.'

Ellen continues: 'I myself understand what she means. The insights are still coming, and the reflections are continuous. I haven't noticed a tremendous change in myself, and I know those around me haven't noticed a change, but I do seem to have opened some kind of a door that was closed before, and hopefully, more will open ... I haven't yet encountered a threatening situation, so I don't know how I will react, but I have had a glimmering of the relief I feel when I am not afraid, and it is wonderful!'

As with many encounter group participants, the change that occurs is a very subtle one and certainly a part of it is a closer acquaintance with oneself and one's feelings. Whether behaviour will alter to fit these newly-owned feelings is in Ellen's mind a real question. As one who has thought about personality theory, I am convinced that any such change in self-perception will inevitably sooner or later show up in behaviour also. Ellen is not so optimistic, as is evident from the following.

In this same letter she tells of having lunch with W, another participant in the group, who had not become very deeply involved. 'He is no easier to know outside the group than inside it. It was really a fruitless attempt at recreating the group feeling. I doubt that there would be that much difficulty with all the others in the group, but probably we all put on most of our shell when we left the Inn.' She concludes her letter: '... our group continues to recede, and the old habits press around again, including the headaches and the rest of the psychosomatic mish-mash. How I wish I could hold on to the group spirit!'

Here is the familiar picture of the group experience beginning to fade in vividness and the old patterns of life reasserting themselves. This is certainly a very common experience of group members.

I replied to her letter, as to all the letters from which I am quoting, but since we were now separated by more than two thousand miles I made no attempt to do anything more than to be understanding of her attitudes, feelings, and situation. I did suggest a therapist in her city to whom she could go if she felt the need.

Mother the Ogre

The next letter is written a month later. For the first time she begins to mention the problem with her mother. She writes from the office, '... mother is out until at least ten o'clock tonight. I am going to see some friends she dislikes and when I get home I *should* simply say I went to visit George and Carol tonight. But I am already quaking with fear that I will get home *after* she does and will not have a ready and plausible excuse for where I have been. This is silly. I know it. But I can't seem to fight it. Therapist, here I come!' She did not, however, go to him at this time.

Her statement about her fear of her mother is more revealing than anything she said in the group and indicates the extent to which she is still a little girl completely under her mother's thumb.

She also talks about the healing element in the group and says, '... the "safe" group where there is nothing to threaten the members seems to be what society needs, what the church could offer if it just had the guts, and what we achieved momentarily in our group ...' She concludes, 'I have ups and downs but I have seen a couple of gains, minute though they are.'

Ellen Thinks about Separation

I answered her letter saying that I hoped she would find the courage to tell her mother where she had been when she visited George and Carol. She replied,

... I am sorry to say I didn't find the courage to tell my mother where I was and I probably never will. As with most human relations, this is far more complex than it may seem, and involves other people as well. I wish I could discuss it with you in detail. Maybe it would help to work things out. Actually, I guess if I didn't feel responsible for my mother's well-being because of her age, I might have the courage, with moral support from my friends, to set up two households. But at 75 she seems too far advanced to just walk out on, although physically she is in great shape and very capable of taking care of herself. How to do it is the question. Even marriage would be difficult, because the one person that could be my mate (George) is also the one person she would like the least – and there is almost no possibility of his being free except through becoming a widower ... His wife is very ill both physically and psychologically. I can only stand by and help if I can, because I am fond of both of them and could never break up what could be and has been a happy marriage. It gets more and more complicated doesn't it? ... However, if I had never known George I would never have had one-tenth the understanding, ability to love, sympathy or tolerance I have now. He made me a human being. And that gave me the ability to feel – joy as well as sorrow. I could bear both, I guess, much more, if I did not also feel the weight of guilt feelings imposed on me by my mother – such guilt feelings, beginning so early in life and culminating in her distaste at the relationship mentioned above. But I must do what seems right for me. Everyone needs to feel needed and loved. I happened to choose a way alien to her. You can see the ambivalence in me. Calvinism vs fundamental human need. Dependence vs desire to stand alone. George had a friend who was a starving poet. He wrote a verse that is not only poignant but very apropos: 'How do we go in our loneliness? One and one. Chant it round with a sigh and a moan. How do we go in our loneliness ...

alone.' I guess we are two of a kind. Maybe that is what brings us together – and keeps us apart.

Here, partly or largely as a result of the encounter group, she is carefully thinking through her immature and cowardly relationship with her mother and facing it. She is also working through the guilt feelings about her one meaningful masculine relationship and is coming to accept her feelings for George.

Daring to Speak – and Choose

By the next letter, only four days later, the situation has shifted quite markedly, and cowardice has changed to courage. She says:

DEAR CARL,

I never meant to involve you to this extent with my problems but I may as well keep you up to date. You can use it as a horrible example some time. A natural opening occurred in conversation with my mother at dinner last night. It was a comment of hers about remodelling the house, which we have been considering. I gently suggested that maybe we should think about neighbouring apartments, so I could go to the conventions and meetings I should be attending without worrying about getting someone to stay with her. She seems to be afraid to stay alone in the house overnight. Naturally, one thing led to another and this morning she was hysterical.

I have talked to the family doctor and got his advice on finding a place – not really neighbouring apartments – I had never intended to do that, really. He reassured me about her attitude, saying (as all my friends have said) that she will speedily adjust, and that it is the only thing for me (how well I know!). There is no turning back now, I am sure. I left her in tears this morning and saying there was no one for her to talk to, and she had no income. This is true. I will simply liquidate as much of our common assets as I can and try to work out a continuing independent income for her. It will have to come partly from my own income.

Much was said – although much was left unsaid, and I could see there would be no understanding or acceptance of it. If I can just keep the courage I have now not to listen to the sobs and keep – as it were – a cold heart in the matter.

As you can imagine, this day is very traumatic for me – a com-

bination of relief that I could do it, and revulsion over the act.
Thanks for listening.

Perhaps we ought just to look at the facts revealed by these
last three letters. Here is a woman forty-four years old who has
been dominated all her life by her mother, who has never married, who is still too terrified to tell her mother of spending an
evening with a male friend (George) whom she loves. She
simply cannot stand her mother's disapproval. Yet five and a
half days in a group, in which this problem was only mentioned
superficially, have somehow set off a chain of independent
thought and action which represents a completely new direction in her life. The fact that this new direction is undertaken
in terror and with a great sense of guilt and enormous insecur-
ity and anxiety does not alter the fact that she has taken a step
from which she can scarcely retreat and which will genuinely
change her whole life style and her conception of herself.

Turmoil

Her next letter, a week later, portrays the upheaval she is going
through with both the good and the bad feelings.

... First there are feelings of guilt and sorrow at what I have done
to my mother. Then there is a kind of burst of 'sanity' like the sun
coming through the clouds, where I think, how ridiculous to be
fearful and guilty about something so natural and normal. And what
harm am I doing to my mother? Perhaps I will be able to get
through the next three weeks in this erratic fashion. Mother will
move into her apartment in three weeks ... Liz, my employee,
assures me that the big adjustment will come when I am on my own,
alone. I am sure she is right. She, as well as my other friends, feel
that once Mother is settled, she will be OK, but that the big question
mark will be my own adjustment. It is the next three weeks that I
am dreading. I am not thinking about the time after that. I get the
guilt feelings like hot flashes. Why? I think I could figure it out.
Reading your book may help. If I can just keep remembering that all
of Mother's concern so far has been for her own being. Very little
evidence of concern about what I am or what I will become.

The old matter of the association with George I mentioned before
still rankles with her. I am sure this is the big specter. And the

reason for my feelings of guilt? I want to be accepted, but feel unacceptable by her – therefore by myself. Is that it?

One week later the outlook is not quite so bleak. 'The next two weeks will be the hardest, I guess, as Mother will be moving, and I will be staying at the house waiting for a customer to buy it. I can't help thinking what wonderful things human beings are. They are tougher than they think. It is the understanding of what is going on inside that is the saving thing. You see, I have become a disciple. Thanks again for your warm notes. You may have a vague knowledge of how much they have meant during this strange and troubling time.'

She met a person who was going to be seeing me and gave her a message, 'Tell Dr Rogers that Ellen is celebrating the Fourth of July.' Her 'celebration' is nearly two months late, but highly significant nonetheless. As evidence of this, she continues, 'I shall not be asking the therapist for help now, I am sure. I think I can get through this OK and with the help from your book and all the wonderful friends who are rallying around both Mother and me I think things will smooth out.'

During this period of turmoil she received a notice of another encounter group programme and suggested to Liz, her staff member, that she should go. Liz 'was thrilled with it but insisted that I should go. She said she was so pleased with the way I was when I came back from the group but that it wore off so soon and she thought that I would profit from this programme so much she felt I should go.' (She did not.)

The Depths

Three weeks later in what she calls a 'regressive state' she writes another letter because she needs to

write it out or fight it out alone . . . I have evidence of nerves today – I am back at the old itching on my arms that I had for years until my doctor prescribed librium two and a half years ago. Which proves something, I guess.

I guess what began this regression after nearly a week of pretty good control was the process of starting to move Mother into her apartment on Saturday. We took some boxes over, and expect to continue doing this, and putting things away until her large items are moved, in about ten days. I have the same old sensitivity to her displeasure and her innuendos about things she doesn't like. The old guilt feelings are back stronger than ever: what am I doing to this poor old 75-year-old woman? And yet I know, logically, that it is not really a terrible thing.

. . . While her apartment is not luxurious, it is comfortable, and in an excellent location. I am doing everything I can to make it attractive. We will be carpeting it, for example. Here I am, trying to convince myself that I am doing the right thing, when underneath I am a quivering mass of fear. Why am I afraid of her? Her most anguished cry last week when she got hysterical again was that I am so cold about it all. I tried to explain that I was not cold inside, but felt terrible, and was merely trying to control my emotions. It all comes down to the fact that I am so terribly afraid of the hysterics, the tantrums, the tongue-lashing, the tears, the accusations. Why? If I could only find the answer to this.

I remember my father once saying to her, 'You sure know how to turn the knife in the wound.' And this surely should be the clue that I don't have to feel guilty – that she has been doing things to me all my life that I didn't recognize until the last few years. Strangely, last week even after the awful hysterics resulting from my selecting an apartment (without her approval) I felt some of the self-confidence that came from seeing the situation for what it is.

. . . I can talk about all the reasons why, but I still can't seem to get rid of that terrible fear in the pit of my stomach, or say anything at home that is going to precipitate the hysterics, the self-pity, the martyr attitude, and the accusations that make the guilt well up in me. I spent yesterday trying to sleep off a tension headache.

. . . Do most 'clients' go through periods of regression like this? I should think they must when they are changing such long-ingrained habits of thinking and feeling. I guess, as both Liz and my cousin Sally keep telling me, the worst is behind. Actually having the courage to open the subject six weeks ago was the big step. If I can only fight down the guilt and the fear!

Many people seem to feel that change in one's self-concept and in one's behaviour can come about smoothly. This is not true in any person, nor is it true of change in an organization. All change involves turbulence and varying degrees of pain, in this case intense pain. When we learn something significant about ourselves and act on that new learning, this starts waves of consequences we can never fully anticipate. It is entirely natural that any such major change in a life-style built on forty-four years of habit formation should cause a period of violent ups and downs – of confidence and depression, of guilt and an occasional feeling of deep satisfaction. Yet the fact that this is natural makes it no easier to undergo, and each individual's struggle is personal and each person has the feeling, especially if the change is deep, of being wildly tossed about like a boat in a storm.

Declaration of Independence

At this same time, in response to a request from the man who had been largely responsible for organizing the workshop of which our group was a part, she wrote a letter trying to sum up something of what it had all meant to her. I received a copy of this letter. In it she summarizes some of her experiences in the encounter group and afterwards.

... As with most of the participants I went to the Inn with a completely erroneous idea of my 'problem'. As you know, our group was an unusually 'healing' one, and it became evident by the sixth day that I had begun to open a door on to my real personal problem, and the entire group did much to open the door. A remark by Carl, and a hope that I would keep in touch with him, went a long way toward the rather dramatic change in me over the past summer.

Something about our group gave me a new concept of the 'precious' quality of the individual. When I got back to the old environment, even the church seemed to be talking in the most unproductive kind of clichés ... The beginning in our group has led to my ability to blend all of these recent experiences into one large insight which resulted in a rather drastic step six weeks ago.

... The drastic step, and the real problem that I took to the Inn under my façade, was the separation of myself from a domineering mother. This is a real casebook problem – it's written up in every elementary psych text. But a life based on fear and submission is not easily changed. I am not yet out of the woods, but the going is easier. I know that our group was the big step, and that I would not yet have been able to face my mother with this break if I had not gained some kind of feeling and understanding about myself and others through that experience.

... I don't know how much you will gain from this letter as an evaluation of the workshop, especially in its purpose of providing people in industry with leadership qualities. But I do hope you will see the emotional influence it has had on this individual, and understand the wonder and hope that I have derived from the experience. At middle age I have finally achieved some degree of maturity. I will begin living a life of *my own* in two weeks, after having provided my mother with the safety and security she needs to live a life of *her own*. Whether she can do it is now up to her – I can't live her life for her any more than she could live mine as she has tried to do . . . So that's about the best evaluation I can give you of the workshop. It helped me find my life.

The Cost of Independence

There was an interval of five weeks before the next letter. In it she says,

Thank you so much for your letter which kept the door open for further correspondence. It helps to write my feelings, but I certainly don't expect you to try to answer each one of my catharses.

. . . You are so right, independence is a costly thing, and I know that I cannot go back no matter how costly. My mother said the first thing about our status last Tuesday night. We were on our way to our weekly bridge session with some friends. She said she couldn't get used to the change and that night time is the worst, and she lies awake for hours thinking about it. It was very difficult to answer her at this point, but I did say, 'Yes, it is hard to make a change. I am having difficulty too. It will take a while to get used to.' She said she would never get used to it and at that I fell silent. I didn't know what else to say. It spoiled the evening and all the next day I brooded about it. I got your letter that day, which helped some.

I am up and down in wildly modulating cycles. Sometimes it seems incredible that this is happening, and I go through the same kind of nightmare experience mother mentioned Tuesday – some day I will wake up and find it is all a dream and I am back again in the former situation. . . . I feel as though I am living in three levels: (1) the 'gut level' that you have spoken about, in which my *being* is doing what is right for it to do; (2) the emotional level in which the dream or illusion of the present is bearing down upon me; and (3) the intellectual level which fights the emotional level and tries to rationalize back to the gut level.

I want to look at this statement from the point of view of a psychologist interested in personality theory. It seems to describe so well the dynamics of personal change. On the one hand she is truly aware, for the first time, of the feelings and reactions of her organism, her 'gut-level' reactions. Her total being is undergoing the new experience of being guided by these reactions and sensing how right this is for her. On the other hand, all the emotions aroused by the accumulation of values introjected from her mother rise up to assail her. 'You are a bad person for deserting and betraying your mother.' 'You are bad not to do what she wishes, to let your life be more important than hers.' 'You are a wicked woman to feel love for a married man.' 'You are bad because you drive her into hysterics.' So the old feelings of fear and guilt and worthlessness and wickedness repeat themselves as in the past. But this time there is a difference. Her *mind* is able to say, 'Yes, I sense the fear and the guilt, but my organism doesn't experience my "badness". It is pleased at the separation from mother, warmed by George's love, and inwardly sad at mother's tantrums.' Her intellect is, as she says, on the side of her organismic visceral reactions – on the side of her *own* experiencing. Thus I am sure the introjected values will come to lose their force.

She continues in regard to her turbulence, '. . . the conflict is devastating. I am dragging physically, tired to death, and not caring much about anything at all. Last week I entertained at dinner for the first time, and had the usual little mishaps of nouveau chefs. But I felt a little bit of enthusiasm. This week I'd just as soon call the whole thing quits – life, I mean. Perhaps next week I will be back on top again . . .'

Fear of Independence

I think the big problem, aside from the worry about Mother, which is actually diminishing, is the fact that I seem unable to stand alone. This is where I must use your book and your approach with every ounce of will in me. I cannot lean on friends, much as I would like to. I miss my good friend, George, who helps me so much. He is extremely busy and involved in a miserable job situation, and I haven't even talked to him in more than a week.

. . . If only parents could realize what harm they are doing their children by doing things for them, not letting them go, not pushing them out when they are reluctant to leave the nest. But I must take some blame, too, for not taking my firm stand long ago and realizing how the starch was going out of me. I am forty-five but feel like a ten-year-old lost in a forest. I know I will find the way out eventually. It is the intervening time that I dread. But one step at a time is all I can take. I try sometimes to visualize what Mother is going through at this point. But everyone, even my pastor, assures me that she is a strong woman and coming through far better than I. And so, except when I see her, I tend to forget any travail she may have, and gloom about my own.

To me it is fascinating to see that the problem has gradually shifted from her guilt about her mother to the recognition that she herself is the problem, that she is having a tremendous time trying to stand on her own feet and live her own life. Here is a fear she is *experiencing*, not introjecting. She is, as she said, paying a high price for her independence and yet it is clear that she is making progress in the struggle. She is squarely facing the fact that she is emotionally ten years old at the age of forty-five. This is quite a step.

She Dares to Confront, and Is Thankful

The next letter came one month later:

Just want to report in to keep my file up to date. I think the last time I wrote I was somewhat depressed. This time I can write on an up-beat note. I think I am doing well. The worst time is having to see Mother over weekends and on Tuesday evening to play bridge. She is not adjusting to her situation and makes little innuendos to let me know how unhappy she is. However, I find that many mothers do this to their children, and I am getting more and more confident about my attitude toward her.

A case in point: My cousin, Sally, asked Mother and me to come for Thanksgiving. She lives only twenty miles away and we go there frequently. We spend Christmas there, too, each year. Last weekend Mother said she didn't want to go to Sally's for Thanksgiving since we were going for Christmas too. The fact that she had already enthusiastically told Sally she would bake pumpkin pies didn't seem to matter. She had that edge to her voice that is so familiar to me. I didn't say anything. A little later she brought it up again, saying she thought she wouldn't go, and if I had something I wanted to do on Thanksgiving I should go ahead and do it. I still didn't say much about it. But when she brought it up the third time I said, 'Mother,

Sally invited me for Thanksgiving, and *I* am going. You may do as you wish.' She simmered down then, and finally said, 'Will you pick me up on Thanksgiving?' Now, really, how childish can an adult be!

I am doing well on my own in the apartment, although I haven't had time to clean the place in a month! I am learning to cook, and had some friends over the other evening whom I haven't entertained for years. It was so wonderful to sit around and drink if we felt like it, and talk naturally – and I was in my own place! My roommate at the workshop was in town last weekend, and we spent a wonderful Friday evening and all day Saturday together. We laughed about getting to know each other finally, since the entire time at the Inn we had roomed together and that is about all. We have a great deal in common, including emotional problems and ideas on what to do about them, and I hope our friendship will continue to flourish.

So – thankful I can be this Thanksgiving! And I hope my mother can find something in her life to make it meaningful, but I know that is not in my power to provide. Best wishes for a happy holiday.

Here, for the first time, she has dared to confront her mother with the fact that she is a separate person. When she found the apartment for her mother it was with much guilt feeling and without much real confrontation. In fact, she left home rather than face the hysterics. Here, however, she says to her mother, 'I am going, you may do as you wish.' She has at last cut the umbilical cord and managed to say (not without some difficulty I am sure), 'I am a separate person from you.' She is now truly celebrating her Independence Day, her Fourth of July. This she states in a letter which arrived a month later.

'. . . The mother problem is gradually working itself out. She clobbers me every so often with the self-pity bit, but I do not dwell on it or allow her to. I realize how difficult it is for her to adjust, and am trying to do as much as I can without entangling myself any more. As far as that situation is concerned, the cord is cut, and never will it be tied again.' All the evidence from her other sources is that her mother is doing well and is quite content.

Another Blow

It would seem as though this very painful and difficult separation, ending in a successful cutting of the cord, was enough of a growth struggle for anyone during a brief period. However, at about this time George, on whom Ellen had leaned very much and whom she loved very much, distanced himself from her psychologically, partly because of his wife's problems and partly by reason of other complications. This as she says in later letters was a 'double whammy in the trauma department'. Her letters tell of the fresh pain of that deprivation and her struggle to face it, but essentially it is the same story all over again. As she notes in one of her letters, a friend told her, 'You do come through the crises remarkably well.' The friend is amazed 'that I have been able to pull out of the second "whammy" so quickly'. In working through a part of this second blow she says:

I felt a sadness as though a baby had died – but it was a grief for a passing *feeling*, rather than for a lost *person*. In the loss of that feeling, I may be opening my life for many more interesting and varied experiences. Instead of wanting to be available for the possibility of his presence I can now freely think of seeing distant friends I have not seen recently ... Searching for genuine affection is a waste of time. If it comes, it comes. If not, I just accept what I have always felt, that I am not particularly lovable because I haven't learned to love properly. Perhaps this realization and acceptance will help me to be more outgoing to everyone and provide some compensation for the lack of a deep personal regard for one individual.

Is the Pain of Growth Worthwhile?

During this period when Ellen was going through her second experience of deep pain, I mentioned in a note to her that she must wish at times that she had never heard of the workshop which got her into our group. She replied, nearly eight months after the original group experience, 'You wonder whether, if I could live over the past nine months, would I be willing to repeat my group experience? In a word, *yes*. The group is precious to me ... It has given me the new dimension to my life that has brought me nearer to maturity ... No, I would not give up the group experience for anything. And even though I have gone through hell many times during these months, I have learned much and am grateful for each of these learning experiences.'

Some Concluding Thoughts

Many people are asking questions these days about encounter groups and their value. These questions, as they might be phrased about Ellen's experience, would include the following: Did it prove an upsetting experience for her? Did it make her unhappy or depressed? Did it cause friction in any of her close relationships? Did it change her attitudes towards man-woman relationships, moving her away from orthodox morality? Did it make her emotionally unstable? Without any doubt, the answer to all of these questions is a resounding *yes!* It proved terribly unsettling; it caused deep unhappiness and depression; it changed her relationship with her mother in such a way as to drive her mother into hysterics; it brought wild fluctuations in her emotional reactions; it caused her to be more acceptant of her loving feelings towards a married man. So it follows, in the minds of those who ask such questions, that her encounter group experience was unfortunate, damaging, and not only of no value but a destructive influence. This kind of superficial judgement has caused many to be both highly critical and apprehensive of the growing place of the encounter group.

But let us look at Ellen's experience from a more significant point of view – her *own*.

The group experience was one of the most precious in her life, a peak experience with caring, 'healing' people, who helped her open doors in her inner life. Pouring into her life came a flood of insights and feelings which helped her open the door, ever so slightly to the experiencing of herself. Yet she was sure the door would close again.

She became openly aware of the domination of her life by her mother on the one hand, and her own complete dependency on her mother — for approval and affection — on the other. She realized how much she feared her mother.

For the first time in her life she began to think seriously about cutting that umbilical cord.

She begins to trust her own feelings — about her man friend, for example, rather than her mother's values and judgements.

She takes the bold step of deciding to move her mother into a separate apartment.

She endures the turmoil, the guilt, the dread, that this decision and her subsequent action bring.

Though it makes her frightened and depressed, she *frees* herself from her mother — first in an inner psychological way, then through the physical separation, and finally through courageously speaking to her as a separate person.

She has slowly grown out of many lifetime habits, and is struggling towards finding her *own* life.

She has lived with the terror of being independent and faced that fear.

She has begun to find moments of deep satisfaction and joy in being a separate person.

She meets deprivation and pain in her love life, but with a new courage.

She has made great strides in the never-ending struggle to become more of a whole person, a person separate but in relationship, a more aware person, a person who at great cost has earned a measure of freedom for herself. And that courage to *be* is so precious that she would go through all the pain again, if need be, to find it.

Her story is not a solitary one. For many others, too, an intensive group experience has proved to be a turning point in the direction of their lives and the nature of their behaviour. But this is a tale of what happened to *one* person, as a result of *one* week in an encounter group.

Quite by accident, I came upon Ellen's correspondence with me some six years following the group experience, and realized what a rich store of personal data it represented and how much help it might be to others going through similar struggles. I wrote to her asking for permission to use non-identifying excerpts, a permission she gladly gave. Then, when I had finished the draft of the above material, I sent it to her, asking her to check it for factual errors and anything she found objectionable. She approved it all, giving some small but helpful additions. In these two recent letters she gives a picture which is, I think, a fitting epilogue to the struggle for growth which has been described. Several excerpts will convey the depth of continuing change in her.

DEAR CARL,

What a strange experience it was to read your manuscript. I felt completely detached, as though I were reading a case study from one of your books. I can scarcely remember some of the emotions I expressed in my letters. How wonderful is a human being – he can forget pain and sorrow. I would not want to go through it all again, yet, having gone through it, I know that I am inevitably better able to meet future crises as a result of having begun to live – really live – my own life. But it does not cause me to feel apprehension, because I know that I can get through the crises. I have proved that.

The relationship with George continued off and on for quite some time following our last correspondence, in an increasingly unsatisfactory manner, until Ellen herself took the initiative in making an open, clean break. 'So I have divested myself of another shackle – years of an emotional dependence that wasn't necessary at all . . . In some ways it was the cutting of a second umbilical cord.'

As to her independent life in her apartment, she writes, 'I have been furnishing it, enjoy collecting art (as I can afford it) and am beginning to do a little creative cooking and a small bit of entertaining. All of this is growing up, you see. I was never taught to keep house, cook, entertain, date, or be a housewife. So I have had to learn everything myself since living alone.

And my work in the business has kept me too busy to do much else.

'Not that everything is great, of course. I still have bad headaches, and think they may be caused by a physical rather than a psychological problem. I am getting a medical examination to find out.'

She tells with real satisfaction of how she has been a helping person in a difficult mother-daughter relationship. The mother, a friend of hers, has been a stiff, formal person who constantly nagged at her daughter for some of her 'hippie' tendencies. Ellen has been able to create a relaxed climate in which they can both express themselves. 'I feel that much of what has happened the past two and a half months is a direct result of what I myself have learned about myself and others in the encounter group. I surely am not as up tight with people as I used to be.'

She continues,

Perhaps most important of all, I have a better image of myself, and while I am not satisfied with myself by any means, I think I can live with my limitations, and simply avoid those situations I know I can't handle. For example, I am not going to many professional meetings where I will be the only, or one of the few, women, and where I don't know the men. There is no point in continually submitting myself to a miserable situation if I don't absolutely have to. Just as I have decided not to make myself drive on mountain roads since they make me sick ... In some ways I am stunted, and probably always will be, just as the reverse is true with some others who became adult in some ways too fast.

It is difficult to imagine Ellen mentioning her mother 'incidentally', but that is the way one of her final paragraphs starts.

Incidentally, my mother is still going strong, and I have begun to admire her strong will to keep active and mentally young. She has a new interest in her revived membership in the social organization to which she has for years belonged, and just made a formal dress to participate in their ceremonies. I can enjoy her company on a weekend, or on a Saturday shopping, although just sitting in her house to chat for more than two hours, including dinner and TV news makes me ready for a tranquilizer. She seems to enjoy coming to my apartment, as a guest, and has been much interested in my decorating (although occasionally a bit appalled at the money I 'waste' on paintings).

CONCLUSION

For me, these recent letters substantiate all I felt could be discerned in the earlier correspondence. Ellen is growing up, as she says, and though the maturing is taking place much later than it might have, the process is still enriching and enlivening her life. She is making her own choices, moving in her own directions, and meeting life very realistically. Can any of us ask for more?

6

The Lonely Person – and His Experiences in an Encounter Group

I would like to start out with a brief statement given to me by a friend of mine after an experience in an encounter group. He writes:

So, here we are, all of us, poor bewildered darlings, wandering adrift in a universe too big and too complex for us, clasping and ricochetting off other people too different and too perplexing for us, and seeking to satisfy myriad, shifting, vague needs and desires, both mean and exalted. And sometimes we mesh. Don't we? (James Flynn, Ph.D.)

My remarks will deal only briefly with the first part of his statement, and focus more directly on the theme: 'And sometimes we mesh. Don't we?' That aspect I wish to explore.

I believe that individuals nowadays are probably more aware of their inner loneliness than has ever been true before in history. I see this as a surfacing of loneliness – just as we are probably more aware of interpersonal relationships than ever before. When one is scrabbling for a living, uncertain as to where the next meal will come from, there is little time or inclination to discover that one is alienated from others in some deep sense. But as affluence develops, and mobility, and the growth of increasingly transitory interpersonal systems instead of a settled life in the ancestral home town, men are more and more aware of their loneliness.

There are two aspects here which seem real to me. The first is the aloneness, the separateness, which is a basic part of human existence. You can never know what it is to be me, and I can never know what it is to be you. Whether we wish to share ourselves quite fully, or hold large areas private, it is still true that our very uniqueness separates us. In that sense every man must live alone and die alone. How he comes to terms with that – whether he can accept and even glory in his separateness – whether he can use his aloneness as a base from which he can express himself creatively – or whether he fears and tries to escape from this fundamental condition – is an important issue but one on which I shall not dwell.

I wish to speak more of the loneliness that exists when the person feels that he has no real contact with other persons. Many factors may contribute – the general impersonality of our culture, its transient quality, its anomie – all elements of loneliness which grow more marked the more we are crowded together. Then there is the fear, which resides in a great many people, of any close personal relationship. These are a few of the factors which may cause an individual to feel he is closed off from others.

But I believe there is a still deeper and more common cause of loneliness. To put it very briefly, a person is most lonely when he has dropped something of his outer shell or façade – the face with which he has been meeting the world – and feels sure that no one can understand, accept, or care for the part of his inner self that lies revealed.

Each person learns, early in life, that he is more likely to be loved if he behaves in certain ways which are approved by his significant others than if his behaviour is the spontaneous expression of his own feelings. So he begins to develop a shell of outer behaviours with which he relates to the external world. This shell may be relatively thin, a role he consciously plays, with at least a dim awareness that he, as a person, is quite different from his role. Or it may become a tough shell or armour plate, which *he* regards as himself, quite forgetting the person inside.

Now when the individual has dropped some of his defensive shell is the time when he is most vulnerable to true loneliness. He may have dropped his façade, or a portion of it, voluntarily, in an attempt to face himself more honestly. Or his defences may have been breached by an attack. In either case this leaves him with his inner, private self somewhat exposed – a self which is childish, full of feeling, with lacks as well as adequacies, and with both creative and destructive impulses – an imperfect and above all a *vulnerable* self. He feels sure that no one could understand or accept this hidden self – an absolute certainty that no one could like or love this strange and contradictory self he has tried so hard to conceal. Hence there develops a deep sense of alienation from others, a feeling that 'if anyone comes to know me as I *really* am, *inside*, he could not possibly respect or love me'. Of this loneliness he is keenly aware.

Let me put it in slightly different terms. Loneliness verges on despair when a person permits himself to realize that the meaning of life does not and cannot reside in the relation of his outer façade to external reality. If I think the meaning of my life can be found in the relation of my role as psychologist to your role as educator or career woman or whatever; if a priest believes the meaning of his life is to be found in the relation of his role as priest to his church as an institution; if the corporation president thinks the significance of his life lies in the relation of his role as president to his executives in their roles, or to his business – then at some point each of these individuals is likely to discover, to his distress, that this is not an adequate basis or reason for living. A striking example is a recent top-ranking Phi Beta Kappa in his college who found his role as grade-getter – no matter how much praise and reward it gave him – utterly empty as a reason for being. No matter how satisfying this façade might be to his faculty, his peers, or his parents, it was a completely unsatisfying basis of existence, and he was brave enough to discover this and honest enough to voice it.

So loneliness exists at many levels and in many degrees, but it is sharpest and most poignant in the individual who has, for one reason or another, found himself standing, without some of his customary defences, a vulnerable, frightened, lonely, but *real* self, sure of rejection in a judgemental world.

The Loneliness Within

There is no doubt that in an encounter group experience the individual often finds a healing for his alienation, his lack of relationship to others. This comes about in various ways. Often the first step is the gut-level experience of the feelings of isolation which he has concealed from himself. One vivid example is that of Jerry, a competent business executive.[1] Somewhat puzzled by the statements of others in the group, he said in an early session: 'I look at myself with some strangeness because I have no friends, for example, and I don't seem to require friends.' In a later session when he heard Beth, a married woman, talking of a remoteness she felt between herself and her husband and how much she craved a deeper and more communicative relationship, his face began to work and his jaw to quiver. Roz, another member of the group, seeing this, went over and put her arm around him and he broke into literally uncontrollable sobs. He had discovered a loneliness in himself of which he had been completely unaware and from which he had been well defended by an armour-plated shell of self-sufficiency.

One young man, a quite self-assured and even cocky individual in his dealings with others, kept a diary of his reactions in a group experience. Here he tells of the point at which he really came to accept his almost abject desire for love, an acceptance of his need for human contact which marked the beginning of a significant experience of change. He says,

During the break between the third and fourth sessions I felt very tired. I had it in mind to take a nap but instead I was almost compulsively going around to people starting a conversation. I had a begging kind of feeling, like a very cowed little puppy hoping that he will be patted but half afraid he'll be kicked. Finally, back in my room, I lay down and began to know that I was sad. Several times I found myself wishing my roommate would come in and talk to me or whenever someone walked by my door I would come to attention inside like a dog pricks up his ears; and I would feel an immediate wish for that person to come in and talk to me. I realized my raw wish to receive kindness.

After this acceptance of his lonely self, his relationships began to change.

Joe, a college student in another group, at one point became

---

1. The example that follows is taken from the documentary film, *Journey into Self*, an Academy Award-winning film available on rental from Psychological Cinema Register, 3 Pattee Library, Pennsylvania State University, University Park, Pennsylvania.

obviously more and more dejected, sitting silent, his head in his hands, his eyes closed, shut off from the group entirely. Previously he had been quite full of zest and life, telling us of the difficulties he was having in running a large project on the campus, some of his anger at not being treated like a person by the college administration, and other current feelings. But then he sank more and more into himself. It took gentle coaxing on the part of the group to get him gradually to open up and reveal what was making him feel so sad. The gist of it was that no one cared for *him*. Some faculty members liked him because he had good marks. Some administrators liked him because he was doing a good job on the project. His parents didn't care for him at all and wished him far away. One particularly poignant statement was: 'Even the chicks I know dig going to bed, but they don't dig *me*.' He had come face to face with the fact that, though his competent student self was well regarded and the things he could do were respected and liked – even to his prowess in bed – still his inner person, his real self, felt unknown, unloved, and uncared for. He had walked head-on into his own loneliness. When some of the group who knew him well put their arms around his shoulder, held him, took hold of his hands, this non-verbal communication gradually got to him and began slowly to convince him that perhaps some people cared for him.

It is not always in an encounter group that one comes to experience one's loneliness. In the sensitive film, 'Rachel, Rachel', the thirty-five-year-old schoolteacher has a constricted, constrained, but seemingly adequate life. The sharpest moment of her discovery of loneliness is when she meets her mother's bridge club with a smiling face, passing out the goodies and greeting each one with her carefully manufactured shell. Then she retreats to her room and weeps her heart out at her complete lack of close contact with any living human being.

'What I Really Am Is Unlovable'

One important element which keeps people locked in their loneliness is the conviction that their real self, the inner self, the self that is hidden from others, is one which no one could love. It is easy enough to trace the origin of this feeling. The spontaneous feelings of a child, his real attitudes, have so often been disapproved of by parents and others that he has come to introject this same attitude himself, and to feel that his spontaneous reactions and the self he truly is constitute a person whom no one could love.

Perhaps an incident which occurred recently in a group of high school girls and some of their faculty members will illustrate the way in which loneliness gradually comes to light and is discovered, by both the individual and the group, and the deep fear even in a person outwardly decidedly lovable that inwardly she would not be accepted. Sue was a rather quiet girl in this group but obviously a sincere and serious one. She was a good student, an effective leader in the organization which had elected her as an officer. Rather early in the week-end encounter she had expressed some of the difficult times she was going through. She had found herself questioning her religious faith, questioning some of her values, feeling very uncertain as to the answers to these questions, and experiencing a certain element of despair. She knew that the answers must come from within herself, but they did not seem to *be* coming, and that frightened her. Some members of the group attempted to reassure her, but this had little effect. At another point she mentioned how frequently other students came to her with their problems. She felt that she was quite available to them and that she found satisfaction when she could be of help to another person.

The next day some very moving feelings were expressed, and the group paused for quite a time in silence. Sue finally broke into it with some highly intellectual questions – perfectly reasonable, but somehow not at all appropriate to what was going on. I felt, at some intuitive level, that she was not saying what she wanted to say, but she gave no clue as to what her real message might be. I found myself wanting to go over and sit next to her, but it seemed a crazy impulse, since she was not in any obvious way asking for help. The impulse was so strong, however, that I took the risk, crossed the room, and asked if I could sit by her on the couch, feeling that there was a large chance I would be rebuffed. She made room for me, and as soon as I sat down she leaped into my lap, threw her head over my shoulder, and burst into sobs.

'How long have you been crying?' I asked her.

'I haven't been crying,' she responded.

'No, I mean how long have you been crying inside?'

'Eight months.'

I simply held her like a child until the sobbing gradually subsided. Little by little she was able to tell what was troubling her. She felt that she could be of help to others but that no one could love her, and therefore no one could help her. I suggested that she turn around and look at the group and she would see a great deal of caring on the faces of those around her. Then one of the members, a nun, told how she had lived through the same kind of period in her own life – doubt, despair, and feeling unloved. Other members of the group also helped. Then Sue revealed that her parents had separated. She had greatly missed her father, and to have a man show a caring interest in her meant a great deal. Evidently by intuition I had acted wisely but I have no idea of how this came about. Here, however, was a girl whom almost everyone would consider a charming and lovable person, yet within, she had seen herself as completely unlovable. My own caring and that of the members of the group did a great deal to change this perception.

In the letters I have had from her since it is very clear that the experience of this love and caring of the group has helped her over her despair. She still has many doubts and questions, but the hopelessness and feeling of being alone and unloved has disappeared.

Taking the Risk of Being One's Inner Self

As is evident in some of these examples, the deep individual loneliness which is a part of so many lives cannot be ameliorated unless the individual takes the risk of being more of his real self to others. Only then can he discover whether he can make human contact or lighten the burden of his loneliness.

For those of you who have seen the film, in 'Rachel, Rachel', this moment comes when Rachel is willing to accept her sexual feelings and give herself to a young man whom she has unquestionably idealized. The love affair is not what one would call a success and she is deserted by her boy-friend, but none the less she has learned that it is only by taking a risk that she can genuinely encounter another human being. This learning stays with her and strengthens her as a person to move out into the unknown world.

I can speak very personally about this because I feel that risk-taking is one of the many things I myself have learned from experience in encounter groups. Though I do not always live up to it, I have learned that there is basically nothing to be afraid of. When I present myself as I *am*, when I can come forth non-defensively, without armour, just me – when I can accept the fact that I have many deficiencies and faults, make many mistakes, and am often ignorant where I should be knowledgeable, often prejudiced when I should be open-minded, often having feelings which are not justified by the circumstances – then I can be much more real. And when I can come out wearing no armour, making no effort to be different from what I am, I learn much more – even from criticism and hostility – and am much more relaxed and get much closer to people. Besides, my willingness to be vulnerable brings forth so much more real feeling from other people in relation to me that it is very rewarding. So I enjoy life very much more when I am not defensive, not hiding behind a façade, but just trying to be and express the real me.

This willingness to take the risk of being one's inner self is certainly one of the steps towards relieving the loneliness that exists in each one of us and putting us in genuine touch with other human beings. A college student expressed this risk very well when he said, 'I felt at a loss today in that encounter group. Very naked. Now everyone knows too much about me; at the same time I am more comfortable in the knowledge that I don't have to put on my "cool".'

The deepest conviction in the lonely person is that once known he would not be accepted nor loved. To see this conviction dissolved in a group is a fascinating part of the process. To discover that a whole group of people finds it much easier to care for the real self than for the external façade is always a moving experience, not only for the person himself but for other members of the group as well.

Take the example of the businessman Jerry, mentioned earlier, who proudly proclaimed that he had no need for friends before he really experienced his loneliness. In one of the closing sessions he said, more haltingly than I can reproduce, 'Well, the first thing I think of is that it is possible to have other people reach out if you in turn will reach out to them. I mean, it is *possible* for this to happen and it is a feeling of becoming closer to people, especially individuals. I don't know why I struggle to say this. The only thing I can relate is this feeling that happened with me regarding Beth's problem and then the response from Roz immediately seemed to take me back into the group – or back into the *human race*, I guess you'd say – back into other people's feelings. They *are* concerned. They *can* be. People can be concerned about you regardless of what type of individual you are. This realization came to me. The thing I will take out of this group is that there is a *tremendous possibility* of this happening, not just here, but *any place* that I try to have it happen.' Not only was Jerry close to tears as he said this, but the members of the group, too, were deeply moved.

There is a profound truth in Jerry's statement that he had been taken back into the human race. It is only as a person discovers that he is loved for what he *is*, not for what he *pretends* to be, not for the masks he hides behind, that he can begin to feel he is actually a person *worthy* of respect and love. This is what puts him in touch with others and keeps him in touch. It is also one of the commonest results of an encounter group where a person comes to have a new respect for the self he truly is. He no longer feels that he is a walking fraud or must continually deceive others in order to be liked. This increased respect and liking for one's self does not always last after the group experience. Sometimes it needs to be renewed. Nor does every member of a group find his loneliness alleviated in the ways described. Yet it does to me seem like a beginning.

I hope these examples help to make clear that in an intensive group experience it is often possible for a person to peer within himself and see the loneliness of the real being who lives inside his everyday shell or role. It is also possible for him to experience that loneliness fully, and find the experience accepted and respected by other members of the group. He can voice and bring into the open aspects of himself of which he has been ashamed or which he has felt were too private to reveal. To his surprise he finds that the members of the group feel far more warmly towards the real self than towards the outer front with which he has been facing the world. They are able to love and care for this real self, imperfect and struggling though it may be. When two such real selves reach out to each other in a group, there is the I-Thou encounter that Buber has so well described. In that instant loneliness is dissolved, the person feels himself in real contact with another, and the estrangement which has been so much a part of his life vanishes.

I am sure there are many other ways of attempting to deal with the aloneness, alienation, and impersonality that exist between individuals in our culture. Sometimes the artist expresses his loneliness in a poem or painting, and expresses also his genuine inner self, hoping that somewhere, sometimes, will come the warmth of understanding and response and appreciation he is seeking. The facing of real danger can also reduce the loneliness people feel. In a war-time platoon or bomber crew – individuals under threat of imminent death – there often comes about a revelation of the true self and an understanding and acceptance of it by others. This accounts for the closeness and intimacy that can exist in these groups, and also for the lifelong nostalgia a soldier may feel towards his buddies after the group has broken up.

CONCLUSION

Doubtless there are other ways in which this loneliness can be allayed. I have simply tried to present one way, the encounter group or intensive group experience, in which we seem to be creating a means of putting real individuals in touch with other real individuals. It is, I believe, one of our most successful modern inventions for dealing with the feeling of unreality, of impersonality, and of distance and separation that exists in so many people in our culture. What the future of this trend will be I do not know. It may be taken over by faddists and manipulators. It may be superseded by something even more effective. At the present time it is the best instrument I know for healing the loneliness that prevails in so many human beings. It holds forth a real hope that isolation need not be the key note of our individual lives.

7

What We Know from Research

This chapter will not attempt a review of the many research studies related to encounter groups, since that task has been admirably and objectively completed by Dr Jack Gibb.[1] He has analysed 106 studies, including seven earlier reviews of such research. He has also examined 123 additional studies which did not measure up to his criteria for inclusion, as well as 24 recent doctoral dissertations from thirteen universities. This is a new development. University interest in the intensive group experience was almost nonexistent before 1960. Gradually the number of university research studies has grown, until 14 dissertations are known to have been completed during the period 1967–9, and many more are in process.

Gibb points out that the frequently made statements about the paucity of research in this field are simply untrue. He found a number of the studies to be of high research quality, although compared with studies made in the psychological laboratory they are more crude, and many of the findings are equivocal.

I would like to quote a number of statements from his conclusions, commenting briefly on each of these from my own point of view.[2]

The evidence is strong that intensive group training experiences have therapeutic effects.

Gibb draws this conclusion from the findings of many studies, and I believe the material given earlier in this volume

1. J. R. Gibb, 'The Effects of Human Relations Training', in A. E. Bergin and S. L. Garfield, eds., *Handbook of Psychotherapy and Behavior Change* (New York: John Wiley & Sons, 1970), chap. 22, pp. 2114–76.
2. The quotations are all from the final section of the above chapter, entitled 'Implications for Practice'.

will bear it out. Personally, I would prefer to say that the group has psychologically growth-promoting effects. This avoids the connotations of a word such as 'therapeutic'.

Changes do occur in sensitivity, ability to manage feelings, directionality of motivation, attitudes toward the self, attitudes toward others, and interdependence.

Each of these terms needs to be understood in the sense that Gibb uses it. Sensitivity implies greater awareness of one's own feelings and the feelings and perceptions of others. It also involves openness, authenticity, and spontaneity.

'Managing feelings' refers primarily to the ownership of one's feelings and the congruence between feelings and behaviour.

By 'directionality of motivation' Gibb is referring to such concepts as self-actualization, self-determination, commitment, and inner-directedness.

'Attitudes towards the self' includes self-acceptance, self-esteem, congruence of perceived and ideal self, and confidence.

Under 'attitudes towards others' he includes decrease in authoritarianism, greater acceptance of others, reduced emphasis on structure and control, and more emphasis on participative management.

By 'interdependence' he refers to interpersonal competence, teamwork in problem solving, and being a good group member.

Since these all commonly constitute hopes of the group facilitator, it is of decided interest to find that the best research to date confirms the fact that changes do occur in these highly significant directions.

The research evidence clearly indicates no basis for making any restrictions as to group membership.

One of the commonest myths regarding groups is that only certain people should be included, or that there should be a careful screening of participants. This does not fit my experience at all. In fact when asked such questions in public I have facetiously replied that I thought very careful screening should be done, and no one should be admitted unless he was a person! I am pleased to see this point of view confirmed by a review of all the available research.

Groups without leaders are effective as training media.

Major studies were done on this at the Western Behavioral Sciences Institute of La Jolla, and the evidence was clear that the group process in leaderless and leader-led groups was very similar. It is, I believe, still an open question whether the leaderless group is *as* effective as the leader-led, but at least it is useful and effective. This finding opens the way to a much wider use of groups. In my own judgement a leaderless group is definitely preferable to a leader-led group in which the leader displays the negative characteristics briefly mentioned at the conclusion of Chapter 3.

To be optimally effective the group training must be relevant to the organizational, family, and life environment of the person.

This is a strong argument for the composition of what Gibb calls 'imbedded' groups, whose members function in close and continuing relationship to each other. This conclusion is strongly supported by my own experience. A closely related conclusion is that

Effective consulting relationships on a continuing basis are at least as important as what occurs in the group sessions in determining impact upon the participant.

This is the point at which many group programmes have failed. A continuing follow-up, suited to the nature of the group and the situation, is of the utmost importance but is rarely carried through. This is one of my own major criticisms of the so-called 'growth centres' which so often provide intensive group experiences for a week-end or a week, with no follow-up whatsoever.

Training experiences to be optimally effective . . . should be concentrated in uninterrupted and continuous sessions.

Again the experience of many facilitators is confirmed that more will be gained in twenty or forty hours of week-end or week-long sessions than in the same number of hours invested in once-a-week meetings. Gibb also makes the point that the total time in the group 'should be longer than it usually is', since research shows greater impact from the longer groups.

Finally,

There is little basis for the widespread concern among lay groups about the traumatic effects of group training.

It is good to see this ghost laid to rest, since not only the layman, but often the psychologist or psychiatrist not involved in groups, can come up with many 'horror stories' about the terribly disturbing psychological effects of groups. In our work with a large school system, described in the next chapter, there were many criticisms and rumours about individuals who had been so upset that they could not carry on their work, etc. When these stories were tracked down, they almost invariably came from people who had not themselves been involved in any group, and the statements were based on what they had 'heard' from vague 'others'. Gibb reports a very careful study of 1200 YMCA directors who had been involved in groups. Rumours were widespread in the organization of 'severe psychological disruption due to the training'. It was found in fact that only four of the 1200 had felt their experience was negative. By the time the investigators reached these four, three had decided the experience had actually been helpful. Only one (out of 1200) still felt his experience to have been a negative one, and he was functioning effectively on the job.

This conclusion is confirmed by my own experience, as I will indicate in citing a survey I made. My own explanation of this 'rumour' phenomenon is that many individuals are threatened by the possibility of change, and they are dimly aware that the major outcome of a group experience is *change*. Thus when they hear that someone wept in a group, or spent a sleepless night, or went through a difficult period afterwards as in the case of Ellen (Chapter 5), they leap to the conclusion that groups are bad and psychologically destructive. Thus they save themselves from being exposed to the possibility of change.

Everyone concerned with the intensive group experience is indebted to Dr Gibb for his concise, thoughtful, and complete analysis of the very large existing body of research in the whole T-group, sensitivity training, encounter group, and organization development field. Those with any interest in research are strongly urged to consult his review.

To give the reader some feeling for very different kinds of research in this field, I would like to present two examples, neither included, for different reasons, in Gibb's survey. The first is a tightly empirical study of the nature of the group based primarily on phenomenological data.

The Process of the Encounter Group

Of the few studies of the nature of the process of change in an encounter group, perhaps the best designed is that carried on by Meador.[3] It was based on a group which met for five sessions in one week-end for a total of sixteen hours, all of the sixteen hours being filmed.[4] There were eight individuals in the group in addition to two facilitators. From the filmed account, Meador selected (in a standardized and unbiased way) ten two-minute segments for each individual – one from the first half and one from the second half of every session. Thus she had ten two-minute sound film segments for each person – eighty such segments in all. The ten for each individual were spliced in random order, not sequentially. Thirteen raters then looked at every segment without knowing whether it came early or late in the process. (In fact, the raters had no knowledge whatever about the group.)

The instrument the raters used in their rating was Rogers's Process Scale,[5] which is a seven-stage scale representing a continuum of psychological activity ranging from rigidity and fixity of feelings: of communication of self; of ways of construing of experience; of relationships to people; and of relationship to one's problems; to flow and changingness and

3. Betty Meador, 'An Analysis of Process Movement in a Basic Encounter Group'. Unpublished Ph.D. dissertation, United States International University, 1969.

4. Basis for the film *Journey into Self*, mentioned earlier.

5. C. R. Rogers, and R. A. Rablen, 'A Scale of Process in Psychotherapy'. Unpublished manuscript, University of Wisconsin, 1958.

spontaneity in these same areas. It was on this Process Scale that the judges rated the eighty filmed segments, following a period of training in its use in which other filmed material was used. It was learned that, though the judges thought they could distinguish early from late segments, they were quite mistaken in these judgements. Consequently, the ratings are truly unbiased and objective. It was not easy to make them, since the scale was designed originally as a measurement of progress in individual therapy, and the raters did not feel at all secure in judgements they were making. Analysis of their ratings showed, however, that there was a satisfactory degree of reliability; that is, they did tend to rate the segments in reasonably similar fashion.

The table (on p. 128) will not have much meaning to the reader unless he understands something of the scale on which the individuals were being rated. Since they were rated at different times from Stage 1 to Stage 6, here are brief and partial descriptions of each of these different stages of process.

First Stage. Communication is about externals. There is an unwillingness to communicate self. Feelings and personal meanings are neither recognized as such nor owned. Constructs are extremely rigid. Close relationships are construed as dangerous.

Second Stage. Feelings are sometimes *described* but as unowned past objects external to self. The individual is remote from his subjective experience. He may voice contradictory statements about himself as an object with little awareness that they are contradictory. He expresses himself somewhat freely on non-self topics. He may show some recognition that he has problems or conflicts, but they are perceived as external to the self.

Third Stage. There is much *description* of feelings and personal meanings which are not now present. These distant feelings are often pictured as unacceptable or bad. The *experiencing* of situations is largely described as having occurred in the past, or is cast in terms of the past. There is a freer flow of expression about self as an *object*. There may be communication about self as a reflected object, existing primarily in others. Personal constructs are rigid but may at times be thought of as constructs, with occasionally a questioning of their validity. There is a beginning recognition that any problems that exist are inside the individual rather than external.

Fourth Stage. Feelings and personal meanings are freely described as present objects owned by the self. Feelings of an intense sort are still described as not now present. There is a dim recognition that feelings denied to awareness may break through in the present, but this is a frightening possibility. There is an unwilling, fearful recognition that one is *experiencing* things. Contradictions in experience are clearly realized and a definite concern over them felt. There is an initial loosening of personal constructs. It is sometimes discovered that experience has been *construed* as having a certain meaning but that this meaning is not inherent nor absolute. There is some expression of self-responsibility for problems. The individual is occasionally willing to risk relating himself to others on a feeling basis.

Fifth Stage. Many feelings are freely expressed in the moment of their occurrence and are thus experienced in the immediate present. These feelings are owned or accepted. Feelings previously denied now tend to bubble through into awareness, though there is fear of this occurrence. There is some recognition that experiencing with immediacy is a referent and possible guide for the individual. Contradictions are recognized as being between attitudes in different aspects of the personality – indicated by statements such as, 'My mind tells me this is so but *I* don't seem to believe it.' There is a desire to be the self-related feelings, 'the real me', and a questioning of the validity of many personal constructs. The person feels he has a definite responsibility for the problems that exist in him.

Sixth Stage. Feelings previously denied are now experienced with both immediacy and *acceptance*. Such feelings are not something to be denied, feared, or struggled against. This experiencing is often vivid, dramatic, and releasing for the individual. There is full acceptance now of experience as providing a clear and usable referent for getting at the latent meanings of the individual's encounter with himself and with life. There is also the recognition that the self is now becoming this process

Ratings of 8 Individuals on Process Scale over 5 Sessions Totalling 16 hours. Adapted from Meador, 1969 (Sessions by Halves)

Individuals	First Session		Second Session		Third Session		Fourth Session		Fifth Session	
	1st half	2nd half	1st half	2nd half	1st half	2nd half	1st half	2nd half	1st half	2nd half
#1	3.2	3.2	3.8	3.1	4.2	3.7	5.6	4.4	4.7	4.5
#2	2.8	2.5	3.2	4.9	2.7	3.8	3.8	3.8	4.8	4.4
#3	3.0	3.0	4.0	3.3	4.2	4.2	4.9	4.5	4.6	5.6
#4	3.1	3.4	3.4	3.5	3.8	3.8	4.6	3.5	3.6	3.8
#5	2.8	2.1	3.6	2.5	3.4	3.8	4.2	3.7	3.8	4.0
#6	3.2	1.7	3.3	3.2	3.1	3.1	5.7	4.7	5.2	4.3
#7	2.5	3.3	3.1	3.3	3.2	2.6	4.5	4.1	4.0	4.4
#8	3.9	4.8	4.7	2.8	4.4	4.3	4.4	5.3	6.0	5.1
Mean	3.1	3.0	3.6	3.3	3.6	3.7	4.7	4.2	4.5	4.5
Mean of each session	3.0		3.5		3.6		4.5		4.5	

of experiencing. There is no longer much awareness of the self as an object. The individual often feels somewhat 'shaky' as his solid constructs are recognized as construings that take place within him. The individual risks being himself in process in the relationship to others. He takes the risk of being the flow that is himself and trusting another person to accept him as he is in this flow.

Findings

The findings of Meador's study, using the rating scale so briefly described, were striking. Every one of the eight individuals in the groups showed a significant degree of process movement towards greater flexibility and expressiveness. They became closer to their feelings, were beginning to express feelings as they occurred, were more willing to risk relationships on a feeling basis, whereas these qualities had not been characteristic of the group initially. As Meador says in a brief article describing her research: 'It is apparent that these individuals, initially strangers, obtained a level of relating to each other not characteristic of ordinary life.' This study gives us a solid picture of at least one facet of the group process.

A Phenomenological Study of Outcomes

A number of years ago, because of the many rumours of psychological damage resulting from groups, I felt I had a professional responsibility to find out if this was true. Over a period of time I made a systematic follow-up by questionnaire of more than 500 individuals who had been in groups I had conducted, or in large workshops for which I was responsible, with other leaders conducting the small groups. Of those contacted, 481 (82 per cent) replied. I attempted to track down some of the remaining 18 per cent and could find no real difference between them and the respondents. Most of these individuals were contacted three to six months following their experience in an encounter group. Two felt that the experience had been mostly damaging and had changed their behaviour in ways they did not like. A moderate number felt that the experience had been rather neutral or had made no perceptible change in their behaviour. Another moderate number felt that it had changed their behaviour, but that this change had largely disappeared. The overwhelming majority felt it had been constructive in its results, or had been a deeply meaningful positive experience which made a continuing positive difference in their behaviour.

I believe this whole survey will have much more meaning if I give the detailed results and personal statements from one of the groups included in this overall study. This is a follow-up study, conducted three to six months following the experience, of a workshop held during the summer session of a university. It lasted five days. There were 110 people, including 50 school counsellors and a number of others in each of the following categories: educators; religious workers; parents. There were several attorneys and an air force squadron commander. Besides those admitted (on a first-come basis), 100 more were turned down, indicating something of the interest in encounter groups.

Certain features of this workshop were slightly unusual. Because a number of the participants were taking summer-school courses in the morning, the workshop began at a noon lunch, followed by a one-hour general session, and then the encounter groups continued through the afternoon and evening, often until midnight. Those who were not attending courses had the opportunity in the morning to watch films or listen to tapes of counselling interviews.

Because the mornings were free for the staff, it was possible to hold a two-hour staff encounter group not only on Sunday evening (the workshop began on Monday), but each morning of the week. By Wednesday the staff was brave enough not only to meet in the morning by itself, but to continue its encounter in the middle of the large meeting room, with the 110 participants clustering closely around. There was considerable apprehension about this on the part of the staff, but it was very rewarding to the participants. (I might add, as a side comment, that this continuing staff encounter group was one of the most moving and growth-promoting aspects of the workshop, since it not only 'opened up' the staff to each other, but made them better facilitators for their groups.)

Here then is the way the participants viewed their workshop experience several months after it occurred. The simple numerical findings are given first, but the more enlightening section, for me, is the freely expressed comments that follow. A full report of the results was sent to each participant.

Follow-Up Questionnaire

Use this page to react freely to the significance the workshop had for you – this may be done in a 'stream of consciousness' manner, organized form, or in whatever way is natural for you. Please be as frank as possible, and feel free to write as little or as much as you wish. *Responses need not be identified.* [The remainder of the first sheet was left blank for the comments and the reactions of the participants.]

Questions

1. As to the influence the *total* workshop experience had on my *behavior*, I feel that the following statements would apply (check any that fit):
   (a) 2 It has changed my behaviour in ways I do not like.
   (b) 17 It has made no perceptible change.
   (c) 1 I behaved differently for a short time, but now this change has completely vanished.
   (d) 34 It made a considerable temporary difference, and some residue still remains as a 22 positive 0 negative change in my behavior.
   (e) I behave differently with:

		positive	negative
34	my spouse, and this change seems	31	3
40	my children, ' „ „ „	33	7
24	my parents, „ „ „	23	1
49	my friends, „ „ „	47	1
62	my co-workers, „ „ „	58	1
47	my superiors, „ „ „	44	2
34	my subordinates, „ „ „	34	0

2. When I consider the impact that the experience of the *small group* had on me, I feel it was:
   (a) 4 mostly damaging, *frustrating* (3) or *annoying* (1) (underline one or more)
   (b) 1 more unhelpful than helpful.
   (c) 5 neutral or made little difference.
   (d) 21 more helpful than unhelpful.

(e) 38 constructive in its results.

(f) 52 a deeply meaningful, positive experience.

(g) 2 so confusing to me that I cannot make a judgement.

3. When I consider the impact on me of the *general sessions* only, I feel they were:
   (a) 0 damaging, confusing, annoying, boring, or otherwise negative.
   (b) 4 neutral, uninteresting, had little impact.
   (c) 16 somewhat helpful.
   (d) 50 constructive, definitely helpful.
   (e) 23 a deeply meaningful, positive experience.

4. As to the influence of the workshop on my awareness of my own *feeling* and others' feelings (check any that apply):
   (a) 29 I have become more sensitive to my own feelings and more perceptive of others; this has been a new experience for me.
   (b) 52 by being aware of my feelings, I have been more open in sharing my 9 positive 4 negative 39 both positive and negative feelings with others.
   (c) 39 I was aware of my feelings before, but not to such a great extent.
   (d) 16 there has been no perceptible change in this area.
   (e) 0 I have become more aware of my feelings, and I wish I hadn't.

Comments

Below are some of the comments in reaction to the questionnaire. They represent the wide range of reactions to the different aspects of the workshop experience.

'Stream of Consciousness'. Most people had overwhelmingly positive responses:

This was one of the most significant experiences I've ever had. It resulted in my feeling more all-of-a-piece about a great many things as well as about people – sort of jelling, cementing of the most positive and helpful attitudes which all my previous living had formed. The most telling word I think, is *freeing*. It was an opening up to wider sensitivity, experience, appreciation of others' experience. Living is much richer. At the time it seemed to be largely emotional, but after these several weeks, I see how it related to my ideas. I believe more deeply in the potentialities for fulfillment as an individual and the potentialities for all mankind.

I still can't believe the experience that I had during the workshop. I have come to see myself in a completely new perspective. Before I was 'the handsome' but cold person insofar as personal relationships go. People wanted to approach me but I was afraid to let them come close as it might endanger me and I would have to give a little of myself. Since the institute I have not been afraid to be *human*. I express myself quite well and also am likeable and also can love. I go out now and use the emotions I have by feeling warm toward people and have learned to love the emotions as a part of me.

For some people the experience was not quite so positive:

In general I found the workshop a considerable disappointment. I expected much more careful selection of the participants. Since this was not the case, the basic encounter groups for me were not helpful. There was too much 'around the campfire' kind of atmosphere. I felt the lack of any real professional setting.

Question 1: *As to the influence the total workshop experience had on my behavior, I feel that the following statements would apply*: (As the reader will note from the numerical count of the questionnaires, many indicated that they behave differently, especially in their relations with others, as a result of the total effect of the workshop. Here are a few of the comments.)

I am more sensitive to my students' problems, more aware of tones of voice which indicate a 'yes, I'd like you to listen' or 'no, I don't want to share this with you'. I have been pleased as friends, colleagues, and students have felt more at ease in telling me how they felt. And I was most pleased when an incident arose with my husband on a trip that he was able to share his feelings with me as I created an atmosphere in which he felt free to express his feelings. And though I do express my feelings much, I gained even more ease in doing so.

I looked forward that Saturday to a new and more meaningful relationship with my wife, of becoming more tolerant and accepting of our differences (values, drives, interests, etc.). I think this happened. She says she noticed a change in our relationship, but I'm afraid I've tended to slip back to the old habits again, although possibly not as deeply as before.

I'm sure there has been a change in my view toward those I work with. Even though this fall has been particularly hectic in opening school, I have enjoyed the challenges, and I think I have been more 'creative' (at least different) in my approach to handling the problems to be faced in my work.

Question 2: *When I consider the impact that the experience of the small group had on me I feel it was:*
(An overwhelmingly majority of the participants felt it was a 'deeply meaningful, positive experience' and 'constructive in its results'.)

An event to which I might refer as a 'second birth'. It brought new life to a life that was headed toward mediocrity or even failure. I can do things (even leave the ministry which I never rationally chose) that previously were out of the question.

While some of it was painful, I was forced to look at myself honestly and to experience a kind of freedom in spontaneous expression of feeling.

Most significant and helpful in facilitating a better understanding of myself and my relationship with others.

Other responses were not quite so positive:

We seemed to get so little done in so long a time. I do feel that if we had had more time it would have been a very meaningful experience.

I feel that I made some good friends in the group. I am not sure that the others even understood my attitudes, my thinking or what I stood for, as a person – even when the session was almost at an end.

One person described the experience as:

Utter frustration – disorganization; uninstructive, disappointing. Unpleasurable experience; stultifying – unstimulating.

And another:

My small group experience was very disappointing because we never got to a place where we really cared for each other. I liked two members especially but actually was never comfortable with the group members. I got bored, restless and very tired. The chairs were awfully hard. I got terribly homesick for my family and wondered why I had come.

Question 3: *When I consider the impact on me of the general sessions only, I feel they were:*
(Again the responses clustered around the very positive with a few responding negatively.)

The greatest value in my opinion of the workshop came from the general sessions.

I have come to find that general sessions of any kind have little long-time meaning for me. The movies clarified some ideas and helped me understand varied approaches to therapy, but I have only a dim memory for the content of the longer sessions.

The model group session impressed me as showing the leaders, in the main, to be honestly 'practicing what they preached'.

I liked the innovation of a staff encounter group, and also having it meet once in front of the whole workshop. I think, though, that it would have been even better if the workshop members had then been able to interact at that session with the staff group. I believe we could have developed at that point a basic encounter among the whole workshop.

Question 4: *As to the influence of the workshop on my awareness of my own feelings and others' feelings:*
(There was a great wealth of positive response to feeling changes.)

I have noticed a marked difference in several areas of my relations with others since the workshop. Perhaps the common denominator is a deepened confidence in myself and my innermost convictions. Since beginning teaching again this fall semester I am happy to discover much more courage in myself to try to live up to my own convictions about teaching (which convictions resemble Rogers' rather closely, I think; hence it takes courage to try to live them!).

Some of the problems which I faced before the workshop are still with me, but I feel different toward them. I feel like they are within my capacity to deal with. Other problems have almost completely disappeared – at least the symptoms. Perhaps the strongest feeling is that of movement toward higher levels of happiness, productivity and inner strength. The important thing to me right now is the feeling of movement – movement in the right direction.

Probably the most rewarding experience of my life. I think I like myself better since the workshop because of the reflection of the group members I see in myself and the reflection of myself I saw in them. Since the workshop my interpersonal relations have been more meaningful and sincere. I've had to laugh at the reactions of others to certain 'open' statements I've made.

Some responses were bittersweet:

Today I am very happy with the results of the five days, but it was not always that way. There was a time that I thought I would never heal. There was a time that it cost me more pain and fear than any other period of my life, especially the first few days after the meetings were over. I was naked to myself. I couldn't stop thinking about what I now knew about myself or what was just coming over the horizon. Even today I am rephrasing and reorganizing what came up then.

During the following sessions up until the last one, I seemed to be learning a skill. It seemed as if I were learning to 'smell' out the true feelings of those in the group. In all my life I have never loved a feeling so much. It would never matter again to me that someone got angry at me as long as it was really the way they felt – as a matter of fact, I would find it somehow satisfying! I came to hate the person who analyzed my feeling objectively like a counselor who is just doing his job but not feeling some things like I was feeling.

A few people had entirely different feelings:

I have attended other workshops of this type and found that in this one I did not change, as I have in others. For much of the time I seemed to be waiting for and trying to help others in the group to get the idea and get moving.

My Own Comment

To my way of thinking, this personal phenomenological type of study – especially when one reads all of the responses – is far more valuable than the traditional 'hard-headed' empirical approach. This kind of study, often scorned by psychologists as being 'merely self-reports', actually gives the deepest insight into what the experience has meant. It is definitely more valuable than to know that participants did – or did not – show a difference of .05 significance from a control group of non-participants, on some scale of doubtful reliability and validity. For me this kind of organized, naturalistic study may well be the most fruitful way of advancing our knowledge in these subtle and unknown fields.

CONCLUSION

I believe it is clear that research studies, even though they need to be greatly extended and improved, have demolished some of the prevalent myths about encounter groups, and have established the fact that they do bring about much in the way of constructive change.

8

Areas of Application

We have, in the foregoing chapters, covered many aspects of the process and outcome of the encounter group and closely allied phenomena such as the task-oriented group, the team-building group, and the like. Implicit in much of what has been written is the idea that the encounter group is applicable to a number of situations. It seems time to attempt to spell that out. I shall list very briefly various areas of modern life in which the intensive group experience seems to have possibilities for constructive use. In most instances these possibilities are already being tried out. This will be followed by a more extensive focus on the one area of which I have the most personal knowledge, namely that of educational institutions.

Industry

The encounter group, or the task-oriented group, has been used in many ways in industrial settings. One of the most imaginative uses has been in dealing with the psychological problems that develop when two companies merge. TRW Systems, Inc. (a very large corporation manufacturing complicated 'space-age hardware') has made extensive use of groups, and one of the ways in which they attempt to handle the problems of a merger includes elements such as the following.

Skilled interviewers from the personnel staff interview all significant leaders in both companies. The purpose of each interview is to determine, 'What are your concerns and apprehensions regarding the implementation of this merger?' One may easily imagine the wide spectrum of concerns which are voiced. In the company being acquired there are, almost always, the issues, 'Will I lose my job?' 'Will they take away all our research money?' 'Will we really be given the chance to function autonomously, or will we be under the thumb of the parent company?' 'I've heard that the president of the acquiring company is a very difficult person to work with. How will we adjust to him?' On the part of the acquiring company the problems are of a different order. 'I wonder if these fellows are really rather incompetent, since their company has not been doing very well.' 'Will they be willing to take suggestions or will they simply be resistant and rebellious?' 'Will we be able to retain all their staff or will it be necessary to drop some?'

Having elicited the various concerns that are deeply felt on each side, the facilitator (employed by the Systems company) brings the two groups together and simply lists on a blackboard the questions that have been voiced. They then proceed to explore more and more openly, as they begin to develop trust in each other, the issues that *really* concern them. This process bypasses all the pseudo reasons for concern which are so often given. It leads towards a frank exchange, better communication, a dissipation of irrational fears to a point where at least the only problems that remain are reasonable and rational ones which have a chance of yielding to some sensible solution.

Another utilization by industry is in what is called organizational development. This does not differ greatly from the personal development which is the goal of most encounter groups. It is, however, focused as much on the health of the organization as on the welfare and development of the individual. Here are the objectives of an organizational development project as given out by the National Training Laboratories:

1. To create an open, problem-solving climate throughout the organization.

2. To supplement the authority associated with role or status with the authority of knowledge and competence.

3. To locate decision-making and problem-solving responsibilities as close to the information sources as possible.

4. To build trust among individuals and groups throughout the organization.

5. To make competition more relevant to work goals and to maximize collaborative efforts.

6. To develop a reward system which recognizes both the achievement of the organization's mission (profits and service) and organization development (growth of people).

7. To increase the sense of 'ownership' of organization objectives throughout the work force.

8. To help managers to manage according to relevant objectives rather than according to 'past practices' or according to objectives which do not make sense for one's area of responsibility.

9. To increase self-control and self-direction for people within the organization.[1]

For those whose primary interest is in industry, and who would like to know more of the ways in which the intensive group experience is used in industrial settings, a group of readings recommended by NTL is listed below.[2]

Churches

Religious institutions have been quick to adopt the encounter group as part of their programmes. Such groups have been widely used in seminaries, with groups of religious leaders, with members of Roman Catholic religious orders, and with parishioners in the churches.

By and large, the main purpose in a religious institution is to build the sense of community which is so often missing from present-day churches, to involve the parishioners in real participation in their own religious thinking and development, and to improve the communication between pastors and par-

1. *News and Reports* from NTL Institute for Applied Behavioral Science, Vol. 2, No. 3 (June 1968).
2. Richard Beckhard, 'An Organization Improvement Program in a Decentralized Organization', *Journal of Applied Behavioral Science*, Vol. 2, No. 1 (1966); W. G. Bennis, *Changing Organizations* (London and New York: McGraw-Hill Book Company, 1966); Sheldon A. Davis, 'An Organic Problem-Solving Method of Organizational Change', *Journal of Applied Behavioral Science*, Vol. 3, No. 1 (1967); A. J. Marrow, D. G. Bowers, and C. E. Seashore. *Management by Participation* (London and New York: Harper & Row, 1967); E. H. Schein, and W. G. Bennis, eds., *Personnel and Organizational Change Through Group Methods: The Laboratory Approach* (London and New York: John Wiley & Sons, 1965).

ishioners, trustees and parishioners, and the older and younger generations in the church.

Government

Thus far, to the best of my knowledge, encounter groups have been used rather rarely in government situations. Mention has been made of the fact that they were used very constructively in the State Department to improve communication between staff members, and to enhance the possibility of communication between ambassadors and staff members and the natives of the host country. This project has unfortunately ceased.

Such groups have also been used in various federal government departments and in groups of high-ranking state employees. Here the purpose has been much like that of organizational development, to open the participants up to a freer, less authoritarian, more communicative type of administrative leadership.

Race Relations

One of the most profound statements that can be made about the encounter group is that it is a means of handling interpersonal and inter-group tensions. I believe it is safe to say that if two groups of people are willing to meet in the same room and talk at each other (not necessarily with), then an encounter group has the chance and the opportunity of reducing the tensions that exist between them. While encounter groups have not been widely used in handling of relationships between black and white or brown and white, there have been a number of encouraging developments along this line, enough to indicate that it is a field of real promise. Ordinarily the first feelings to come out in such groups are those of incredibly deep bitterness on the part of minority group members. It is only when these have been talked out and accepted by the facilitator, and gradually by other members of the group, that progress can be made towards deeper understanding.

It should be clearly stated that the use of encounter groups is not simply a means of dampening down tensions so that the situation is quieter. If this were the result, it could be in the long run a very harmful thing. Instead, the deeper understanding I have seen emerge in such a group often culminates in positive action steps, which are agreed upon by all concerned and which give a basis for constructive community steps towards alleviating the worst obstacles to racial equality. In my mind, there seems no doubt that, instead of merely a few, there should be hundreds of such groups involving all our racial minorities, black, brown, red, and yellow, with members of the establishment – the police, average citizens, government representatives, the extremist.

This is an area in which the use of encounter groups holds enormous promise, but has been thus far very little developed. Undoubtedly part of the difficulty is due to the trouble of financing such ventures, but part of it also is the fear individuals have of meeting at close range other people whose attitudes and feelings are quite different from their own.

International Tensions

Here I can comment only briefly, since I know of no real attempt to utilize this procedure on an international level. The State Department experiment comes closest to it. I would like simply to voice one fantasy. We are all too familiar with the meeting of two diplomatic teams, one from each government. Each is committed to the line it is instructed to follow; there is little room for individual freedom of expression, and only very limited freedom for negotiation. If, in addition to the diplomatic delegation, each government would appoint several citizens of equivalent calibre who would not be bound by any 'party line', these two informal groups could meet together as persons, not as representatives of set points of view. As *persons* they could explore their differences, their bitterness towards each other, the insoluble problems they face, the attitudes of resentment and fear – the whole range of differences that divide the two national groups. Based on our experience in other areas, it would be only natural to expect that out of this initial exploration, probably full of tension at first, would come an

increasing number of insights and a much deeper understanding of each others' point of view and the reasons for it.
Ideally, the facilitator for this group should be a trained person
belonging to neither country.

Then, if the views of the informal groups could be fed to the
official delegations, this might open the way to new channels of
realistic negotiation at the official level. This is based on the
view that the informal groups would be meeting as persons,
not as delegates, and as persons would try to communicate
with and gradually understand one another.

Families

Enough has been said in previous chapters, I believe, to indicate that encounter groups may help to resolve or prevent many
marital tensions. Among engaged couples with profound
differences in attitude and values – which often exist – these
can be brought to light, explored, and either reconciled or ac-
knowledged as a basis for dissolution of the engagement. With
married couples, if tensions could be explored before they are
suppressed into explosive judgemental attitudes, there would
be a much greater hope of marital harmony. In family groups,
the communication between parents and children could be
greatly enhanced through the services of a facilitator able to
extend understanding to both age levels. Such understanding
might also be extended across families, so that if children could
not communicate with their own parents they could at least
communicate with other parents in the group. The same would
be true in reverse for the parents.

Generation Gap

Closely allied with the foregoing is the need for encounter
groups to bridge the so-called generation gap. In groups where
there has been a wide spread of age, it has not been found that
these age differences are of any significance once the group
process really begins to operate. I recall very well one group in
which the age range was from 17 to approximately 65.
Towards the end of the meetings one of the older members

asked somewhat apprehensively of the younger ones, 'Have we been a detriment to the progress of the group? Do you wish that the group had been composed entirely of younger people?' The response was one of surprise on the part of the young people. They said, 'After the first hour or two, you weren't old or young. You were George, or Mary, or Al, or whoever you are as a person. Age didn't seem to make any difference.' I think this provides a clue as to how the generation gap can be bridged, provided both young people and their elders are willing to expose themselves to such an experience.

Educational Institutions

In our schools, colleges, and universities there is a most desperate need for more participation on the part of learners in the whole programme, and for better communication between faculty and students, administrators and faculty, administrators and students. There have been enough experiments along this line so that we know it is perfectly feasible to improve communication in all these relationships, and it is nothing short of tragic that education has been so slow to make use of this new social invention.

Because I am more familiar with the functioning of the group in educational institutions, my illustrations will be from that source.

A number of staff members and I, at the Center for Studies of the Person, have tried this new instrument for social change in a large educational system consisting of a women's college which trains many teachers, eight high schools, and fifty elementary schools.[3] The system is staffed and supervised by the Catholic Order of the Immaculate Heart, and its top leaders wanted very much for us to come in and help them introduce a process of self-directed change. Without this strong support from the top we would not have embarked on this venture. Administrative support is most necessary.

Jointly with a committee from that system we planned a

3. This whole experiment is described at greater length in chapter 15 and in the epilogue to my book, *Freedom to Learn* (London: Charles E. Merrill and Prentice-Hall, 1969).

series of encounter groups for college faculty, college students, and eventually a variety of groups of faculty *and* students. Finally, the administrative council of the college which, like most administrators, is reluctant to get involved in personal things, requested a task-oriented group and helped find the leaders for it. We also held separate encounter groups for high school faculties and high school students and then finally with high school faculty, administration, and students *together*, although the faculty had been quite apprehensive at first about meeting directly with the students. We held a large number of workshops with the staffs of the elementary schools: teachers and principals. These groups ranged from being somewhat disappointing to the participant to outstandingly successful groups in which everyone, including the facilitator, found much personal profit in the experience.

One of the changes achieved was in the administrative structure and policy of the organizations, particularly the college. As a result of the task-oriented workshop, the budget system and the way the budget was set up were completely overhauled to make it much more participative and not an imposed budget. Several serious interpersonal frictions and problems in the administrative council were worked out – with deep feelings and a few tears – in a way which left things running definitely more smoothly. Jointly, the administrative council planned an all-day session between the students and the president of the college in which the whole point was to hear what the students wanted, their aims for the college and for themselves, and their criticisms of its present functioning. This proved a most profitable undertaking, in the judgement of all concerned.

There also developed all kinds of innovative changes in the classrooms. For one thing, we began to receive many invitations to meet with teachers and students in a particular course, or with a department faculty and the students majoring in that area. Almost without exception, these sessions turned out extremely well, and faculty-student communication was greatly improved. Particular teachers and departments have also introduced many, many innovations. I think these have all been in the direction of greater student participation and initiative; more self-responsibility, self-discipline, and deeper

cooperation between faculty and students. Such changes have
gone on in the teaching of languages, philosophy, teacher education, music, theatre arts, an interdisciplinary seminar involving scientists – almost the whole range of the college
curriculum. Not only have these innovations taken place, but
they are still continuing more than three years after the experiment began, even though we as outside facilitators have withdrawn entirely.

Perhaps one example taken from a recent letter will indicate
the sort of thing that is still happening. 'We are working on a
self-initiated and self-directed programme in teacher education. We had a fantastically exciting week-end workshop
here recently. Students, faculty, and administration, 75 in all,
brainstormed in a most creative and productive way. One outcome is that students will immerse themselves in schools all
over the city observing classes, sitting in on faculty meetings,
interviewing teachers, students and administrators. Our students will *then* describe what *they* need to know, to experience, to do, in order to teach. They will then gather faculty and
other students around them to assist them in accomplishing
their own goals.' Here is self-directed change at its best.

One of the significant outcomes which made this last experience possible was that the system became so convinced of the
value of the intensive group as a means of self-directed change
and problem-solving that they sent several of their people
away for training as group facilitators, and these people are
now able to assist with task and encounter groups within the
system itself. A senior administrator is the next to undertake
such training.

It might be interesting to note the history of this project. The
proposal was first drawn up in early 1966. All attempts to get
funding from the Office of Education and from foundations
failed, and I was at a loss to know what to do. I decided that
the idea was sound, that it needed to be tried, and so the
proposal was published as an article in an educational
journal.[4] This led to strong interest on the part of several
school systems and eventually to the funding of the project by

4. 'A Plan for Self-Directed Change in an Educational System', *Educational Leadership*, Vol. 24 (May 1967), pp. 717–31.

the Mary Reynolds Babcock Foundation and Charles F. Kettering II. Hence it was possible to carry it through. Yet, even as recently as 1966, it was regarded as an utterly impractical and unwise experiment by all the major funding agencies: the Ford Foundation, the Office of Education, and others.

Project Transition

In view of the difficulties we had in initiating this project, it is heartening to learn of a much larger one, following in general the same purposes but profiting by our mistakes and better and more broadly planned and much better funded. This is 'Project Transition' in the schools of Louisville, Kentucky. Here is a description of the situation faced by that school system:

The Louisville District at present has 60,628 children in the District; 35,454 are white and 25,174 are black; 34.1% are from families with annual incomes of $2,000 or less or who are receiving welfare. Most of these low-income students are concentrated in the inner-city schools, and a large proportion are black. These figures represent a tremendous increase in both black and low-income students for the Louisville District in the past 20 years. In Kentucky, the Louisville District has the greatest number of low-income students (20,678), the highest number of under-achievers (71% are below the national averages), the most pupils dropping out of school (second highest rate nationally among large cities), the most delinquency referrals (nearly 5,000), the most delinquency apprehensions (600), the highest student and teacher turnover (approximately 20%, excluding transfers within the District), the greatest number of unemployed (13,900, or nearly one-third of the state's total), and the highest level of racial isolation due to shifting housing patterns . . . [5]

In the face of this very serious educational situation, indeed crisis, bold new plans were devised. The school board, consisting of three whites and two blacks, publicly pledged itself to meet the needs of the city's school population. A new superintendent was employed who had had experience in encounter groups and training in behavioural science processes. He was

5. Quoted from the proposal submitted by the Louisville schools to the Office of Education with figures corrected as of 1969–70.

committed to a full-scale involvement of all school personnel and community groups in a totally new programme in the schools. He was able to secure research and consultant support from local universities in the area of Louisville. He also obtained generous support from the Office of Education, showing the difference that four years can make in the attitudes of a government agency.

In brief, the project is divided into two interrelated components. First, an organizational development programme which uses a series of week-end encounter groups (on paid time) for administrators, teachers, trustees, and some parents, to improve communication and encourage a high degree of participation in policy and programme decisions by all persons within the school organization or served by the schools. The second phase is the encouragement of local school teaching staffs to propose programmes they believe would improve the educational effectiveness of their own school: through more relevant curricula, differentiated staffing patterns, humanistic teaching processes, or flexible educational structuring. One of the major purposes of the whole programme is the 'retraining of teachers to provide interpersonal skills to be used in establishing more supporting and empathic relationships with pupils'. Another is the 'creation of racially balanced faculties which will develop living models for improved human relations'.

A strong follow-up component is built into the whole programme. In addition to the communication laboratories and human potential seminars, weekly training sessions will be continued for fifteen sessions for all top-level administrators, to help them to a better understanding of group dynamic processes and the management of conflict, team building, and development of improved interpersonal skills.

I recently visited this school system and was enormously impressed by the progress they are making in getting this important project under way. They are going to focus their attempts first on 14 schools, six of which will be a very special focus of the project. As they learn from their experience in these schools they will attempt to broaden the sweep of the programme. When I met with the superintendent, Dr Newman Walker, I found him a person with a deep understanding of the enormous change he was attempting to bring about in the schools and a full recognition of the fact that this would undoubtedly produce turbulence and criticism before the project was completed. I also met with the school board, and found that they, too, were fully aware of the risks they were running but nevertheless were determined to bring about a change in the educational system. Perhaps their attitude is best indicated by the fact that at the meeting I attended, a group of the student presidents of the different high schools met with the board to propose drastic curriculum changes in their schools. The board members not only listened attentively and receptively but finally adopted the suggestion that, since the students had made so much progress in such a short period of time in bringing constructive suggestions to their attention, they would pay them for a period during the summer to really complete the job of surveying the situation and making a much more complete body of recommendations.

How is it possible to attempt a bold and venturesome project like this in a city which would not normally be thought of as an experimental community? The reasons are both interesting and to some extent discouraging as well as heartening.

In the first place, the Louisville city school system is composed almost entirely of inner-city schools, where the problems are really tremendous and something must be done. No one can deny the urgency of the situation.

The kind of parents who might be most likely to object if their children were not getting a standard education have moved out to the suburbs, and hence parental resistance is reduced.

The school board seems truly representative of the inner city and is well aware of the urgency of the problem with which they are faced.

The superintendent has had experience conducting an experimental programme for school drop-outs; he has actually had experience of encounter groups; hence, he is convinced at a gut level that this approach has something to offer.

The Office of Education, typically several years behind the times, is now ready to finance a large experimental undertaking of this kind.

All of these factors add up to the possibility of an exciting process of change in an entire school system. The community is large but not enormous; it is still manageable. The experiment can be tried on a broad enough scale to really test it out. The project is bold and radical in the best sense, meaning that it is attacking the very roots of the problem in our educational system rather than the symptoms. It is tackling in head-on fashion the most difficult problem in modern life: the educational system of the underprivileged urban community – the problem of the inner-city schools.

It will not surprise readers of earlier chapters in this book that I predict, as change is brought about, an increasing degree of turbulence and criticism in the whole educational system. Whether the faculty and administrators will be polarized remains to be seen. At least there will be ample opportunity to talk out differences and explore new alternatives if those first tried seem unsatisfactory. It is the boldest and most promising venture I know of in educational systems at the present time, and many people will watch it with great interest.

I think this 'Project Transition' shows that where there is a will to be experimental, the encounter group can be used in depth, the follow-up process can be carried through, and the possibility of change is greatly enhanced. Undoubtedly the opportunities are just as great in all the fields I have mentioned, although few except industry have gone as far as this particular city and board of education.

9

Building Facilitative Skills

How can the number of skilled facilitators be kept in some sort of reasonable relationship to the rapidly increasing number of people interested in participating in groups? A well-informed leader in the field estimates privately that during 1970, 750,000 individuals will participate in some type of intensive group experience. While there is no way to check the accuracy of this figure, it would seem a reasonable guess. Where will the facilitators for these groups come from? It is an urgent problem. We need such leaders for all the areas of application described in the last chapter. It is my purpose to present and discuss one important attempt to meet this need.

The La Jolla Programme

That undertaking is the La Jolla programme of the Center for Studies of the Person, the organization of which I am a part. I select it for presentation for several reasons: I regard it as a unique programme, differing in many ways from most training programmes; I can be reasonably objective about it, because I had no part in its initiation and play a very minor role in it; and finally, its policies make a great deal of sense to me, and I hope they may be followed more widely.

At this writing the La Jolla programme is entering its fourth season, and by the end of the summer of 1970 will have provided significant learnings for more than six hundred potential facilitators who are involved in one way or another with back-home groups. The three co-directors of the programme are Dr Bruce Meador, Dr William Coulson, and the Rev. Douglas Land. The background of these men includes both education and experience in such varied fields as counselling, pastoral counselling, clinical psychology, psychotherapy, group facilitation, education, philosophy, philosophy of science, theology, and administration. They have gradually developed a clear-cut yet flexible policy for providing experiences which will build facilitative skills, leadership skills, and new methods of personalizing educational processes, encouraging inventive freedom on all occasions of human interaction.

Philosophy and Policy

Most basic to the programme is a point of view centred in the relationship of persons to persons. One of their announcements states this well:

Permeating the program – in the style of leadership exemplified by the majority of the staff and also presented in the content sessions – is a person-centered philosophy of group leadership, a view which emphasizes that there is maximum growth for both group and facilitator when the facilitator participates as a *person* in his group rather than as any sort of expert.

This philosophy explains why every effort is made to avoid the word 'training' (and why I have omitted it from the title of this chapter). 'Training' implies making a person proficient in some trade or art or work which he can then use occupationally. But one cannot 'train' an individual to be a *person*. It seems most unfortunate that for historical reasons (explained in Chapter 1) many facilitators of groups are called 'trainers'. To the extent that they live up to this term they are, in my judgement, unfitted to be with intensive groups. So the La Jolla programme emphasizes the humanness of the person who is perceived as the facilitator, and the fact that he is the more *effective* as he is more *real* in his interaction with others.

All this means that the quality and atmosphere of the La Jolla programme is informal and personal, with distinctions between staff and participants kept to the absolute minimum. I realize that this statement may be misunderstood. The knowledge and experience of the staff member is in no way hidden from the participant. He knows, for example, that embarrassed silence is a characteristic of the beginnings of a group, and regards this neither as privileged information nor as background he must share with the group. He is a staff member, but he is first of all a human being.

Growing out of these general beliefs is another distinctive feature of the programme. So far as humanly possible, the staff completely avoids putting any formal stamp of approval on those who have participated in the programme. There are no diplomas, no certificates, no written guarantee of any kind that the participant has now become an 'expert'. It is the hope and belief of the staff that a person leaving the programme will be somewhat better qualified to deal with any of his back-home groups than he was when he came. That is the total goal. These back-home groups may be classes, staff organizations, family constellations, or groups labelled as encounter groups. There is no intent, however, to establish the participants as encounter group gurus!

One of the reasons for this strongly held policy is that it is simply impossible to guarantee that every participant will become an adequate group facilitator. If he has no diploma to put on his wall, no certificate of expertise, individuals will judge him for what he is and will make the decision as to whether he is helpful to a group. If he is not, there will be little demand for his services. He cannot awe people by his diploma.

Closely related to this whole policy is the fact that little attention is paid to the paper credentials of those who attend. Thus, there are Ph.Ds in various fields, MDs, and individuals who have not completed college. They are all on equal footing as persons.

With this summary of the background philosophy let us turn to a more factual description of the programme itself. Although programmes of one, two, three, and four weeks have been tried, the present judgement of the staff is that three weeks is the most satisfactory length. Partly for logistic reasons, the number in any three-week programme is limited to about a hundred. Three such programmes are held each summer, when it is usually easier for busy people to find the time to participate.

Selection

The participants are largely self-selected, though preference is given to those who are already dealing with significant groups. By and large, the summer participants hold positions of influence in American institutional life, numbering among them college deans, elementary school administrators, college presidents, a large cadre of classroom teachers, psychologists, counsellors, members of industry (often from personnel departments), some college students, and chaplains and ministers of a variety of denominations. In addition, each summer brings a small foreign contingent. There is a small but increasing number from the health professions and from the general public.

Elements of the Programme

Though the programme varies from year to year and is always open to change, three continuing elements have been present from the first: experience as a participant in more than one small encounter group; cognitive sessions, exposing the participants to a wide spectrum of approaches used in groups; and the opportunity actually to co-facilitate two week-end encounter groups.

Let me describe in somewhat more detail these three elements. Of the 150 hours spent in the programme itself, about half this time is given to direct experience in encounter groups. The staff of facilitators for these groups is selected largely from leadership on college campuses – those who have had extensive experience as facilitators, including at least one summer La Jolla programme. Recently the attempt has been made to give the participants experience in more than one encounter group, these new groups being formed in various ways. This provides several learnings. It helps the participant to realize there is no magic about the make-up of his first group, and that the process is not one which could only work with those particular individuals. It acquaints him with the sadness of parting from persons with whom he has been very close. He also comes to realize that even a second or third group starts slowly, with much the same tentative milling around that marked the beginning of the first, though every member has just come from a meaningful encounter experience. One cannot hope for 'instant intimacy' but must build trust once more. Another by-product of this change in groupings is that it gives each person a wider acquaintance with all the participants in the programme.

Last year the staff experimented with the concept of community meeting – frequent and intensive meetings for the entire community of participants, a development which it was felt would have particular application to their back-home settings. This proved definitely successful, indicating that once participants have had an encounter group experience it is possible for the close and intimate climate of such a group to permeate even a much larger community.

I recall vividly one such meeting at which I was privileged to be present. The whole community of over ninety persons became a live and deep encounter group. Tension between two of the leading staff members had been experienced by the participants, but not understood, and they encouraged the two individuals to bring these tensions into the open. Soon the whole group was deeply involved, as painful and embarrassing experiences were first tentatively, then openly and tearfully shared. The healing efforts of the community were as noteworthy as the expressions of the staff members, which revealed them for what they were, imperfect human beings. A large number of persons undoubtedly can, in proper circumstances, become a united encounter group, as unitary as the usual small group. It is to the credit of the La Jolla programme that its leaders are learning how to achieve this.

The cognitive part of the programme is shaped in part by the needs and wishes of the participants as they develop and is thus variable from programme to programme. However, it has usually included talks and discussions and demonstrations such as the following:

Theory and Demonstration Sessions
The facilitation of a demonstration group and discussion of same
How I facilitate a group (others and I have participated in this)
A person-centred model of leadership
Structured approaches to groups

Classroom simulations as a learning approach
Psychodrama
Theory building in relation to groups
Applications to Inter-racial Work
Research Backgrounds and Needs
The Relationship to the Drug Scene
The Process of Community Building
Special Problems of Application in
    Educational institutions
    Counselling
    Religious institutions
    Families

The third element of the programme, co-leadership of week-end encounter groups, has been a bold, exciting, and on the whole remarkably successful enterprise. Participants in the programme who feel ready to co-lead a group are urged to select a partner, and the two of them sign up indicating their desire to meet with a week-end group. Announcements are sent out to many persons and institutions in the larger San Diego area and throughout Southern California, indicating that there will be week-end workshops at low cost. The only charge is a small registration fee and living expenses. (In the announcements it is made perfectly clear that the facilitators are persons in training, which is the reason for the lack of any tuition fee.)

When the staff of the La Jolla programme first planned such an enterprise I did a little arithmetic and confronted them with what I thought was the foolhardiness of their venture. I told them I thought they would need between five and six hundred persons to provide enough membership for the groups; that it was almost impossible to get together that number without accidents, both physical and psychological; and that they were taking a very great risk in letting their participants try out their skills on such a large scale. To my amazement, six hundred people showed up for the first week-end and eight hundred for the following one. This is somehow, to me, a measure of the almost desperate need people feel for greater intimacy and communication. In the first three years of the programme approximately eight thousand people have been involved in these week-end groups, and the follow-up reactions have been almost uniformly favourable, and often deeply enthusiastic. Sometimes the experiences in these week-end groups have seemed better than those of groups conducted by much more practised hands.

In all of the eight thousand persons engaged in these groups to date, there has been no psychological breakdown of any kind during the week-ends. There have been, much later, two instances of a psychic break in participants in the programme. It is a question whether this is more than would normally occur in any equal number of the population over the same period of time.

As I have puzzled over the sometimes astonishing success of these week-end groups, I have seen some elements which are perhaps important in group facilitation. The co-leaders, with varying degrees of experience ranging from none at all to considerable, have been continuously in one or more encounter groups for two weeks before they undertake their first week-end programme. This means that they are opened up to their feelings, more aware of themselves than usual, and much more immediately accustomed to the full use of themselves as persons. When they meet with a group of strangers to foster the development of a group process, they are consequently about as completely 'present' as it is possible for an individual to be. Each is a human being, trying to get in touch with himself and to participate with others as the person he is. He comes through as being somewhere between where he started from and the goal he is moving towards. He involves himself freely in this week-end of search, struggle, and adventure. I believe this openness, awareness, and receptivity – this genuineness and spontaneity – are one of the reasons that nearly all these week-end groups have been very successful indeed.

Perhaps another element is the very fact that the facilitators-in-training are not 'experts'. People tend to be intimidated by someone they perceive as an expert. Here they have been explicitly informed that the leaders are not experts, and so members can more readily come out from behind their masks. Also they feel more responsibility for the group. *Reciprocal* help is noteworthy. The facilitator is endeavouring to be of use to the group, but group members also feel free to come to his rescue when they sense that he is not being facilitative. Thus, more growth occurs on both sides.

The programme ends with the last part of their experience in building skills; the co-leadership of a second group. Thus, the training gives them a substantial amount of experience as well as both personal and cognitive input.

This co-leadership of week-end groups is possibly the most important part of the programme. The facilitator-in-preparation has learned in his own small group that he can be deeply, personally touched, and can open himself to change. Now, in the week-ends, to learn that he can be the occasion of others being equally touched, equally opening themselves to change, is something very potent as well as humbling. He leaves knowing that he can create an occasion for growth.

One criticism which might be made of the week-end programmes is that the numbers are too large for follow-up, except in the limited sense achieved when participants who come for one week-end return in considerable numbers for another, either that same summer or later on.

Back-Home Relationships

Especially during the latter part of the La Jolla programme, a great deal of emphasis is put on the way the experience may be utilized back home. Participants are encouraged to apply their learnings from the summer weeks to the settings in which they already find themselves, rather than attempting to set up new encounter groups. They are helped to think through how to use the skills and attitudes acquired in the summer inventively and imaginatively in the much-needed task of making institutional life more personally relevant to those involved in it. Attention is also paid to the question of how family life can acquire more of an encounter group atmosphere. It is the belief of the staff that unless this summer experience improves the functioning of the individual in his own environment, among the people and groups with whom he is already involved, it has not fully succeeded in its purpose, though it may have provided him with a most enriching experience during the three weeks.

There is as yet no way of measuring how successful they have been in achieving this goal, but the continuing and growing demand for the programme indicates that participants feel they have been helped in this way. Certainly, most of the applications for future programmes come from personal contact with someone who has already participated. This appears to be a good sign.

CONCLUSION

In my judgement this programme runs somewhat sharply counter to many of the leadership programmes now being operated in various parts of the country. It de-emphasizes the manipulative, interpretative, highly specialized expertise which appears to be more and more prominent in the training of group leaders. It does not greatly stress the 'exercises' which have become such a large bag of tricks for many group leaders. Instead, it concentrates largely on the development of persons who are more effective in their interpersonal relationships, both during the programme and in their back-home situation. Both its background philosophy and its approach to building more facilitative persons is worthy of consideration by all who have a part in this burgeoning field.

10

What of the Future?

Some Possibilities

With the mushrooming development of groups, what does the future hold in regard to the group movement itself, and what implications for the future of our institutions and our whole cultural milieu? While I do not fancy myself as a prophet, I will endeavour to look as deeply as possible into my cloudy crystal ball. Let us consider first the general trend towards the development of groups. What are some of the directions it may take?

In the first place, I must acknowledge that it may all too easily fall more and more into the hands of the exploiters, those who have come onto the group scene primarily for their own personal benefit, financial or psychological. The faddists, the cultists, the nudists, the manipulators, those whose needs are for power or recognition, may come to dominate the encounter group horizon. In this case I feel it is headed for disaster. It will gradually be seen by the public for what it would then be: a somewhat fraudulent game operating not primarily for growth, health, and constructive change, but for the benefit of its leaders.

Another related and equally disappointing possibility is that, because of excessive zeal and the use of more and more 'far-out' procedures by leaders and facilitators, it may be condemned by the man in the street without his ever looking at the more solid and positive core of the trend. Already I am told that groups focused on personal growth are losing enrolment to those where the drawing card is the charisma of the leader, or the opportunity for much body contact with members of both sexes, and the like. To the extent that this development takes precedence, 'encounter group' may come to be a dirty word, just as 'progressive education' did years ago. It may be worth our while to look at the parallel. Because progressive education became ultra-popular and was carried on more and more by extremists and by those with little or no understanding of its basic principles, it became anathema to the public, and educators were careful to deny that their schools were examples of it. I know of no educator today who would state publicly that he stands for progressive education. Therefore it *seems* to have died out. Meanwhile, the roots of almost every innovative change in education in the last several decades can be traced back to the thinking of John Dewey and to the principles which were in fact the underlying guides for the best of progressive education.

I can envisage the same thing happening to encounter groups, sensitivity training, T-groups, and all the rest. They would become objects of condemnation and die out. Meanwhile, all the essential elements – the building of trust in small groups, the sharing of self, the feedback, the sense of community – would continue to find labels and guises by which they could operate to bring about the changes and communications we so desperately need.

A somewhat more ominous possibility is that the whole trend might be well repressed by a society which seems increasingly antagonistic to change and definitely does not value the individual freedom of thought and expression, the spontaneity, the changingness, and other personal qualities which emerge from an encounter group. Currently the possibility of a take-over by the extreme right seems more likely in this country than a take-over by the extreme left. But the encounter group movement would be ruled out of existence in either case, because rigid control, not freedom, would be the central element. One cannot imagine an encounter group in present-day Russia or even Czechoslovakia, though there is ample evidence that many individuals in those countries yearn for just the kind of freedom of expression it encourages. Even less can one imagine an encounter group being held in a chapter of the John Birch Society, or the Minutemen, or the Ku Klux Klan, or any other organized right-wing group. No, the encounter group can flourish only in a basically democratic environment. If there is a dictatorial take-over in this country – and it becomes frighteningly clearer that it might happen here

– then the whole trend towards the intensive group experience would be one of the first developments to be crushed and obliterated.

Being optimistic and hopeful by nature, I cannot spend too much time on these gloomy visions. Certainly another of the real possibilities is that the whole surge towards groups may continue to grow rapidly and soundly, and to spread its influence ever more widely. What then? In this case we will, I think, see a proliferation of forms. I am not prescient enough to suggest more types than we already see in incipient form and which have been mentioned in this book: groups focused on the building of teams, on the development of true community, on deeper growth of sensory awareness, on meditation, on creativity. I am sure there will be many, many more, with differing foci, but maintaining many of the essential qualities of the encounter group. These will be the new ways of 'turning on', of living life vividly and fully without the use of drugs.

We will most assuredly see far more imaginative procedures to help the person to behave differently but realistically in his back-home situation. These will include not only a more specific focus on this problem within the group, but also many types of follow-up. There will be lists of 'action steps' which a person plans to take, and on which he can be consulted from time to time. There will be meetings of the group itself at some future time – not trying to recreate the glow of the initial encounter but to assess seriously the changes, if any, that have resulted. There will be follow-ups by exchange of cassettes, by regular consultation, by visits of facilitators to group members 'on the job', whether at home or in industry, education, the church, or wherever. In short, there will be ingenious approaches to nourishing the individuation, insight, and self-confidence which began in the group.

We will, I believe, see a more formless spread of the encounter group *spirit* and *climate*. Barbara Shiel has given us an example of what this might mean in a sixth-grade classroom,[1] and I have learned to develop the same climate in a graduate seminar. There is no organized encounter group. There is

1. See Chapter 1 in C. R. Rogers, *Freedom to Learn* (London: Charles E. Merrill and Prentice-Hall, 1969).

simply freedom of expression – of feelings and thoughts – on any personally relevant issue. It takes somewhat more imagination to envisage what an industry or a college might be, if permeated by this climate. And when one thinks of a bureaucracy such as the Bureau of Indian Affairs, or the State Department, it takes a vivid imagination indeed! Yet it is not necessarily impossible. Will a person-centred organization *always* be a contradiction in terms? I believe not.

We shall continue to examine some of these possibilities as we look more deeply at some of the implications for the future.

Implications for the Individual

Here again I can only project into the years ahead trends which I already see in the present. It seems clear that the encounter group movement will be a growing counter-force to the dehumanization of our culture. We live in an increasingly impersonal milieu formed by scientific technology, industrial technology, and urban crowding, as well as simply the 'hopeless bigness' of our cities, industries, and multiversities. Allied with these factors is the deterministic behaviourist view of a man as only a machine. Another element is the increasing computerization of industry, government, education, and even medicine. This is not necessarily bad in itself; it simply keeps underlining the depersonalized image the person has of himself as a mechnically filed and stimulated object, dealt with by utterly uncaring machines and bureaucrats.

Here the encounter group has deep implications. The more the movement spreads – the more individuals experience themselves as unique and choosing persons, deeply cared for by other unique persons – the more ways they will find to humanize our currently dehumanizing forces. The individual will no longer be simply an IBM card or a series of facts stored on a memory-tape for a computer. He will be a person, and will assert himself as such. This is certain to have very far-reaching effects.

Similarly, the encounter group can be an attempt to meet and overcome the isolation and alienation of the individual in contemporary life. The person who has entered into basic encounter with another is no longer completely isolated. It will not necessarily dissolve his loneliness, but at least it proves to him that such loneliness is not an inevitable element in his life. He can come in meaningful touch with another being. Since alienation is one of the most disturbing aspects of modern life, this is an important implication.

There is, it seems to me, an even broader future significance in intensive group experience for the individual. It is an avenue to personal fulfilment and growth. When material needs are largely satisfied, as they tend to be for many people in this affluent society, individuals are turning to the psychological world, groping for a greater degree of authenticity and fulfilment. As one participant said, 'It has revealed a completely new dimension of life and has opened up an infinite number of possibilities for me in my relationship to myself and to everyone dear to me. I feel truly alive.' This goal of living life more fully, of developing one's possibilities in all their richness and complexity appears to be one of the major satisfactions towards which man is turning. Of the many diverse experiments by which he tries to experience a fuller range of life, the encounter group is already an important element and is likely to become more so in the future.

One of the narrower but highly significant possibilities is the chance given by intensive group experience of exploring new solutions to the problem of the man-woman relationship. What are we to do about marriage, when in some parts of Southern California three out of four marriages end in divorce? What are we to do about the children of those marriages? What is the future of the family? These basic issues will not be solved by admonitions, laws, or intellectual discussion. New answers may be developed, however, as men and women, both before and after marriage, explore, as deeply as they are able, their own interpersonal relationships and what they wish to make of them, in the close *experience* of a group. Here too, especially in family groups, there can be exploration of the relations between parents and child, the deficiencies in that relation, and experiments and solutions to be tried in the future.

Significance for Our Culture

Conceivably one of the most important implications of the encounter group is that it helps the individual in adapting to change. Very few people seem to realize that one of the most basic questions for present-day and future man is the question of how rapidly the human organism can adapt to the almost unbelievable speed of the changes brought about by technology. Toffler, in an excellent article, refers to this as 'future shock', suggesting that people will simply collapse in attempting to adapt to the incredible changes brought about. One of his illustrations seems to me very striking. He points out that man's existence can be seen as perhaps eight hundred lifetimes of sixty-some years, extending over a period of fifty-thousand years. 'Of these eight hundred, fully six hundred and fifty were spent in caves. Only during the past seventy lifetimes has it been possible to communicate effectively from one lifetime to another – as writing made it possible to do. Only during the past six lifetimes have masses of men ever seen a printed word. Only during the past four has it been possible to measure time with any precision. Only in the past two has anyone anywhere used an electric motor. And the overwhelming majority of all the material goods we use in daily life today have been developed within the present, the eight-hundredth lifetime.'[2] Thus, our technology is forcing upon mankind a rapidity of change for which the human organism is poorly prepared. Certainly the encounter group with its various offshoots and related groups is an enormous help in enabling individuals to become aware of their feelings about change, and to make of change a constructive possibility. This is why some of the central chapters in this book have been devoted to *how* people and organizations change. This problem seems likely to grow ever more pressing as time goes on, and surely anything that helps man to adjust to change will be highly significant.

A closely related way in which the encounter group may help us to meet the future is as an instrument of institutional change. For the future will demand no less in the way of institutional change than of personal change, and here the various

2. A. Toffler, 'Future Shock', *Playboy*, Vol. 17 (February 1970), p. 97.

institutional applications discussed in the last chapter may be highly important. Unless government, the schools, churches, industry, and the family can react with great alacrity to the necessity of change, we are indeed a doomed culture. What we need in fact is not changed institutions but a *changingness* built into institutional life: an instrument for continued renewal of organizational form and institutional structure and policies. Thus far some of the offshoots of the encounter group movement come closer to achieving this than anything else I know.

The future may need even more urgently than the present an instrument for handling interpersonal and inter-group tensions. In a culture torn by racial explosions, student violence, insoluble international tensions, and all types of conflict, such an instrument for the improvement of gut-level communication is of the utmost importance. Like other new social inventions, this one has been tried all too seldom in intense situations, but if the future is to deal with such conflicts with any success it must greatly enlarge the use of this tool. I can say that our staff has worked with many types of tensions – inter-racial controversy; conflict between students, faculty, and administration; conflict in labour-management situations – and it is only fair to conclude that here is a partial test-tube solution to such situations. The question for the future is, can we try it on a larger scale?

The Challenge to Science

An exciting question for the future is the challenge posed by the encounter group to science. Here, most clearly, is a powerful and dynamic phenomenon. Science has always advanced by studying such potent situations. But can we develop a *human* science capable of adequately exploring the real and subtle issues that emerge from the dynamics of an encounter group? Thus far I feel that the research – hard as individuals have worked on it – represents only feeble and essentially outdated attempts. Students of the subject have, with rare exceptions, been anecdotal – as I have tended to be in this book – or minutely empirical, coming up with 'hard' findings of no real significance. The challenge is to develop a phenomenological human science which will be realistic and illuminating for this field of human activity.

How will this come about? I have no answer, but I can put forward a suggestion. *Suppose we enlisted every 'subject' as an 'investigator'!* Instead of the wise researcher measuring changes in his subjects, suppose he enlisted them all as co-researchers. There is now ample evidence that the so-called naïve subject is a figment of the imagination. The moment a person becomes the object of psychological investigation he starts developing his own fantasies as to the purpose of the study. Then, depending on his temperament and his feeling for the researcher, he sets out either to help develop the finding he *thinks* is wanted, or to defeat the purpose of the study. Why not bypass all this by making him a member of the research team?

Let me try to make this more concrete by giving a recent fantasy of mine as to how the process of the encounter group, and the process of change in the individual, might be more deeply or humanly studied.

Assemble a number of people without encounter group experience. Tell them explicitly that in addition to the experience we wish to enlist their help in finding out more about it. Then at the end of each session or day, each person could be asked two types of questions, dictating his responses privately and briefly into a tape recorder. Something of this order: '(1) Do you feel you are exactly the same now in your feelings, reactions, attitudes, insights, and behaviour as you were at the beginning of this session? If so, simply say so. If, however, you detect changes, no matter how small or large, describe them as best you can and also tell what to you seemed to be the reason, the cause, of these changes. (2) Do you feel the group is just the same as it was at the beginning of the session? Again, if so, simply state this. If you feel the group has changed in some way, describe this change or these changes as best you can and tell why you think they occurred.'

A research worker would immediately begin a preliminary analysis of this material, looking for similar or contrasting themes from the participants on both the individual and group dimensions. The last day of the group could be spent in having these central themes of change or non-change fed back to them and asking for their discussion of this raw material. I believe that out of some such procedures would come a deeper *knowledge* and *insight* into the process of change in the group than we have at present.

I am not at all disturbed by those who would say, 'But this is not science!' When studies are unbiased, communicable, and replicable, they are science, and I have confidence that we could learn more significantly about many human mysteries if we wholeheartedly enlisted the intelligence and insight of the person involved.

This is not to say that this is the only answer, but it may be one small channel by which we can feel our way towards developing a science more adequate to the study of the human person.

Philosophical Values

The encounter group has a clearly existential implication in its increasing tendency to emphasize the here and now of human feelings and of living one's life. This existential quality reflects much of the current development in our philosophical thinking and actual living. It illuminates the philosophical stance of Maslow and May, and of some of their illustrious forerunners: Kierkegaard and Buber. It is consonant with the exciting theatrical development of a stage performance like *Hair*, which aims for a new type of immediate personal involvement in the theatre, and bears a relation to what is happening in art and music and literature. I do not feel competent to spell this out fully, but it is apparent that in a world which is living by an increasingly existential philosophy the encounter group will have much to contribute.

Finally, this type of group as it develops in the future should help to sharpen and clarify the values we hold for man himself. What is our model of the human being? What is the goal of personality development? What are the characteristics of the optimum human being? I am sure it is evident from the thrust of this whole book that in a climate of freedom and facilitation group members move towards becoming more spontaneous, flexible, closely related to their feelings, open to their experience, and closer and more expressively intimate in their interpersonal relationships. This is the kind of human being who seems to emerge from an encounter group type of experience. Yet such a model goes directly contrary to many religious, cultural, and political points of view and is not necessarily the ideal or goal towards which the average man in our society would wish to move. Here is an issue which needs the full and open consideration of the future. We have an opportunity to choose the kind of person we will create.

CONCLUSION

I trust this chapter has made clear that the whole movement towards intensive group experience in all its forms has profound significance, for both today and tomorrow. Those who may have thought of the encounter group as a fad or phenomenon affecting only a few people temporarily would do well to reconsider. In the troubled future that lies ahead of us, the trend towards the intensive group experience is related to deep and significant issues having to do with change. These changes may occur in persons, in institutions, in our urban and cultural alienation, in racial tensions, in our international frictions, in our philosophies, our values, our image of man himself. It is a profoundly significant movement, and the course of its future will, for better or for worse, have a profound impact on all of us.

Index

More about Penguins
and Pelicans

Penguinews, which appears every month, contains details of all the new books issued by Penguins as they are published. From time to time it is supplemented by *Penguins in Print*, which is a complete list of all titles available. (There are some five thousand of these.)

A specimen copy of *Penguinews* will be sent to you free on request. For a year's issues (including the complete lists) please send 50p if you live in the British Isles, or 75p if you live elsewhere. Just write to Dept EP, Penguin Books Ltd, Harmondsworth, Middlesex, enclosing a cheque or postal order, and your name will be added to the mailing list.

In the U.S.A.: For a complete list of books available from Penguin in the United States write to Dept CS, Penguin Books Inc., 7110 Ambassador Road, Baltimore, Maryland 21207.

In Canada: For a complete list of books available from Penguin in Canada write to Penguin Books Canada Ltd, 41 Steelcase Road West, Markham, Ontario

During the last twenty years America has witnessed the birth of 'humanistic psychology'. Stemming from a desire to rethink traditional behavioural psychology, it aims to understand and help, within a less strictly scientific framework, the complex and irrational human being.

Psychotherapy and Existentialism *Victor E. Frankl*
The Doctor and the Soul *Victor E. Frankl*

'The views which Dr Frankl put forward both here and in his other writings represent the most important contributions in the field of psychotherapy since the days of Freud, Adler and Jung. And his style is far more readable.' – Sir Cyril Burt.

The Farther Reaches of Human Nature *Abraham Maslow*

Abraham Maslow, who died in 1970, was a leading thinker in the human potential movement. His strongly held belief that value-free science was 'unsuitable for human questions' helped to revolutionize traditional behavioural psychology.

Gestalt Therapy *Frederick Perls, Ralph F. Hefferline, Paul Goodman*

The authors of this volume and founders of the Gestalt psychotherapy, believe 'that the Gestalt outlook is the original, undistorted, natural approach to life; that is to man's thinking, acting, feeling.'

Joy *William C. Schutz*

This book simply and attractively shows how members of encounter groups are brought face-to-face with their defences and cultivated responses and are enabled to break them down.